my WORLD

LONDON, NEW YORK, MUNICH, MELBOURNE, DELHI

DORLING KINDERSLEY
Editorial Lead Heather Jones
Senior Editors Ros Walford, Michele Wells
Senior Art Editor Ann Cannings
Designers Ian Midson, Clive Savage
DTP Designer David McDonald
Senior Production Controller Rachel Lloyd, Charlotte Oliver
Associate Publisher Nigel Duffield

PRENTICE HALL
Senior Technology Editor Alexandra Sherman
Video and Photography Production Manager Neville Cole
Lead Designers Judith Pinham, Sarah Aubry
Lead Editors Salena LiBritz, Mark O'Malley

10 9 8 7 6 5 4 3 2
002-177813-Jun11

ISBN: 978-0-7566-8343-6

Color reproduction by MDP UK
Printed and bound in China by L.Rex Printing Co. Ltd.

Discover more at
www.dk.com

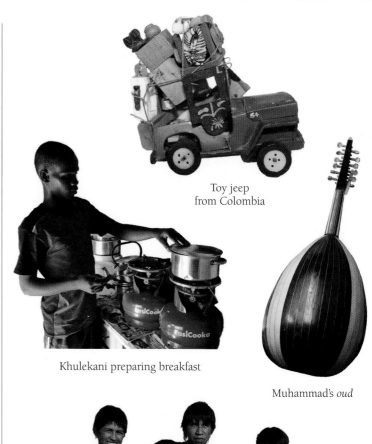

Toy jeep
from Colombia

Khulekani preparing breakfast

Muhammad's *oud*

Omar and his
soccer team

Nancy making
pickles

Contents

Luis saddling up a horse

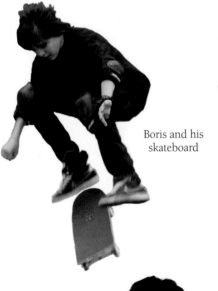

Chinese fish
and vegetables

Boris and his
skateboard

Askar playing
keyboards

Carolina with her
school friends

Maayan's MDA
Volunteers badge

Yasmin learning
martial arts

Alyssa's Inuit doll

Jack's Maori
pendant

Bilal at the
water pump

My World, *My Story*

Yasmin

These real-life stories feature teens from 22 diverse countries of the world, from the Arctic to the Equator. Some of them come from privileged backgrounds, while others endure hardships in their daily lives. Boris, for example, is an award-winning skateboarder from Russia; Omar works in a Bolivian mineral mine; Nancy from India wants to join the police. Although uniquely shaped by their environments, they share a commonality that unites teens everywhere—they like sports and music, are proud of their cultures, and enjoy spending time with family and friends.

North America
UNITED STATES

Vy

North America
CANADA

Alyssa

North America
MEXICO

Carolina

North America
DOMINICAN REPUBLIC

Luis

South America
COLOMBIA

Daniella

South America
BOLIVIA

Omar

South America
BRAZIL

Vinicius

Africa
GHANA

Evelyn

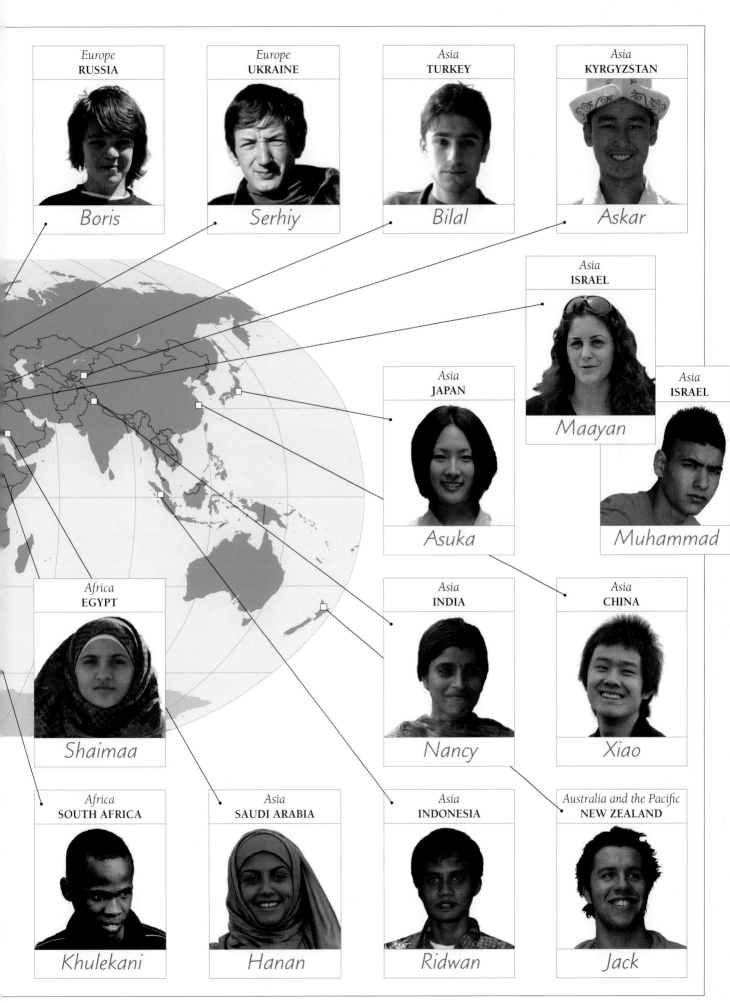

Europe
RUSSIA

Boris

Europe
UKRAINE

Serhiy

Asia
TURKEY

Bilal

Asia
KYRGYZSTAN

Askar

Asia
ISRAEL

Maayan

Asia
JAPAN

Asuka

Asia
ISRAEL

Muhammad

Africa
EGYPT

Shaimaa

Asia
INDIA

Nancy

Asia
CHINA

Xiao

Africa
SOUTH AFRICA

Khulekani

Asia
SAUDI ARABIA

Hanan

Asia
INDONESIA

Ridwan

Australia and the Pacific
NEW ZEALAND

Jack

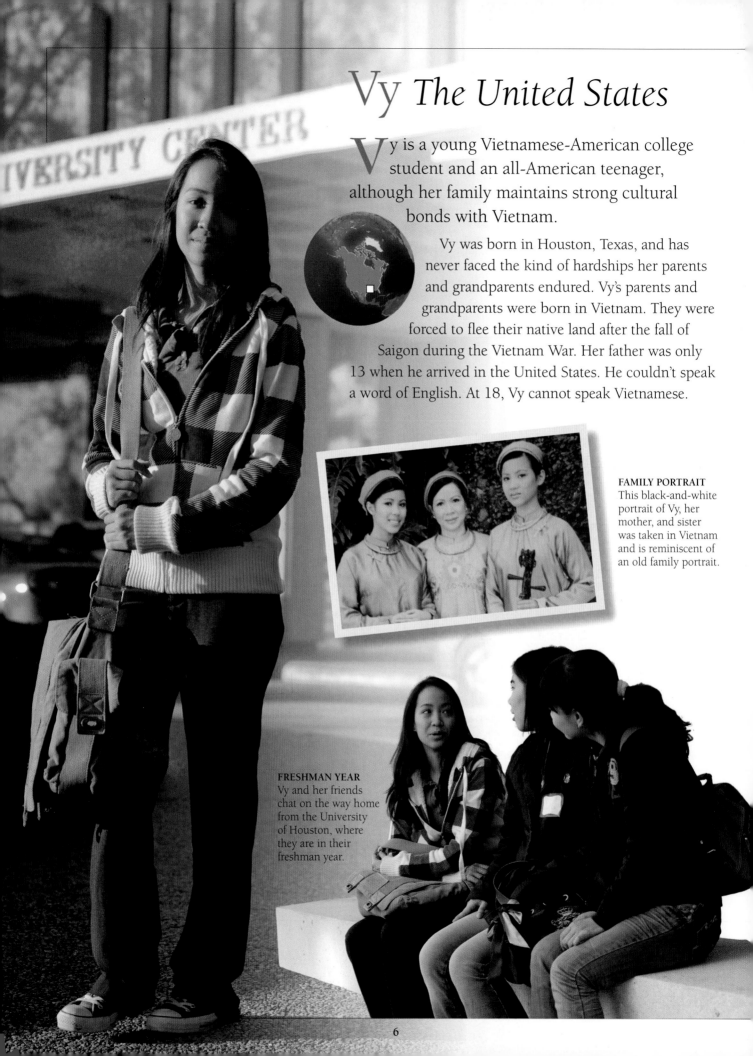

Vy *The United States*

Vy is a young Vietnamese-American college student and an all-American teenager, although her family maintains strong cultural bonds with Vietnam.

Vy was born in Houston, Texas, and has never faced the kind of hardships her parents and grandparents endured. Vy's parents and grandparents were born in Vietnam. They were forced to flee their native land after the fall of Saigon during the Vietnam War. Her father was only 13 when he arrived in the United States. He couldn't speak a word of English. At 18, Vy cannot speak Vietnamese.

FAMILY PORTRAIT
This black-and-white portrait of Vy, her mother, and sister was taken in Vietnam and is reminiscent of an old family portrait.

FRESHMAN YEAR
Vy and her friends chat on the way home from the University of Houston, where they are in their freshman year.

HOUSTON, TEXAS
Houston is a large multicultural city.

"I think so many people here take for granted that they can do what they want and say what they want. That's a choice not everyone gets to make in other countries."

Vy

WORKING DAY
Vy balances academics with a job in her father's business.

Despite Vy's ancestry, Vietnam is a foreign and faraway place to her. She is entirely at home in the United States. Vy is one of 36,000 students who attend the University of Houston—the second-most ethnically diverse national university in the country. As a freshman, she is trying to balance academics with a job at her father's business, DI Central, a computer-related data company. She currently assists the marketing department by compiling information about customers and contacting those customers to conduct satisfaction surveys. She has yet to declare a major but thinks she might follow in her father's footsteps by focusing on business.

Quick to acknowledge her parents' tremendous sacrifices, Vy's greatest fear is letting them down. She feels she has been given luxuries her parents never had and should be even more successful than they've been.

Vy has her own car and her own cellphone, but she admits nothing is more important than the freedoms found in America. "I think so many people here take for granted that they can do what they want and say what they want. That's a choice not everyone gets to make in other countries," she says.

LUXURIES
Having a car gives Vy freedom that she does not take for granted.

Such freedom has allowed Vy great independence. At the same time, she refuses to bury her family's roots and seems driven by her heritage. She has left behind her interest in high school sports to focus on college. Her textbooks and laptop now consume afternoons once spent at the mall. "My day starts at my dad's office at 9 A.M. and most nights I don't get home until 7 or 8. I don't really have the free time that I used to." When she does have time to herself, she draws comic strips to express her feelings and plays ping-pong with her dad—a fierce opponent who, she jokes, takes the game too seriously.

ATHLETIC ACHIEVEMENTS
Growing up, Vy won medals for volleyball and basketball.

LEISURE SPORTS
A favorite method of relaxing is playing ping-pong with her dad.

Vy still lives at home. She shares a very close relationship with her two older sisters and younger brother. She credits her mother with maintaining a strong cultural bond. Her mother prepares traditional Vietnamese meals, with beef and fish dishes, and she insists the family eat together.

HOMEWORK
When she gets home at night, Vy spends time doing her homework.

TRADITIONAL COSTUME
Vy and her family pose in traditional Vietnamese dress in this photo, taken when they were in Vietnam.

EATING TOGETHER
Vy's mother cooks traditional Vietnamese dishes for all the family to enjoy together.

MEMENTOS
Vy and her family took lots of photos as mementos of their trip to Vietnam.

"I just couldn't wait to get home and have a cheeseburger."
Vy

Three years ago, Vy took her first trip to Vietnam. Her family spent a month touring the country. The experience was bittersweet. "The cities were so dirty and so crowded, and the people seemed to have so little," says Vy. "I almost felt guilty that I had so much."

Although she still finds it impossible to imagine what her parents endured, it's a trip she says she will always treasure. Visiting Vietnam allowed Vy a unique opportunity to learn more about the land her parents call home, but she is quick to confess, "I just couldn't wait to get home and have a cheeseburger."

WALKING THE DOG
Vy and her sister Ly walk the family dog in their neighborhood.

Alyssa *Canada*

Alyssa is from the Canadian province of Ontario. Her family is Inuit and she enjoys learning about the traditions of her culture.

During the Spring in Ottawa, Canada, the ice melts, the grass begins to grow, and the city's waterways flow freely. Most Canadians begin to enjoy the beautiful outdoors of the nation's capital. But 20-year-old Alyssa heads north in the Spring to visit her extended family in the snowy city of Iqaluit in Nunavut. In the 1950s some of Alyssa's family, including her mother, Martha, were relocated from Inukjuak, in northern Quebec, to Grise Fiord, near the Arctic Circle. It is Canada's northernmost community, earning it the Inuit name of *Aujuittuq*, meaning "place that never thaws."

FAMILY ALBUM
An old photograph of Alyssa as a baby being carried by her mother.

ICE HOUSE
Alyssa with her aunt in an igloo at Iqaluit in the far north of Canada.

CAPITAL CITY
Located in the province of Ontario,
Ottawa is the capital city of Canada.

Canada's indigenous
populations are diverse, and
Alyssa is a prime example of that
diversity. Her mother's family
is Inuk Inuit, and her father is
Cree. The Inuk Inuit people are
often labeled "Eskimos." Alyssa
considers the term "Eskimo" not only
incorrect, but disrespectful. "Eskimo,"
interestingly, is a Cree word, which means
"eaters of raw meat." Alyssa explains, "There
is an indigenous population in Canada, and within
that population there are three different groups. There are
Métis, First Nation, and Inuit. Specifically, I am Inuit. The Inuit
are native to Canada's northern regions. The First Nations are
indigenous tribes that receive governmental support, and Métis
are people who have mixed backgrounds of indigenous and
French or Scottish heritage. It is a bit complex, eh?"

"ITK is a national organization for Inuit,
and it works on environmental, health,
and socio-economic issues for Inuit."
Alyssa

OFFICE WORK
Alyssa enjoys her work for Inuit Tapiriit
Kanatami, an organization for Inuit people.

LUNCHTIME
Alyssa treats her
coworkers to
a traditional
Inuit lunch.

A few days later, back in Ottawa, Alyssa jumps into
her work at the Inuit Tapiriit Kanatami (ITK), which
means "The Inuit Brotherhood of Canada." "ITK is
a national organization for Inuit, and it works on
environmental, health, and socio-economic issues
for Inuit," says Alyssa.

On one particular day, several of Alyssa's
coworkers gather in the break room.
Alyssa has brought caribou, narwhal, and
arctic char fish from Iqaluit. Coworkers
have planned a "Country Food" luncheon.
"We don't have the opportunity to do this
all the time, since we live in southern
Canada. So this is really nice," beams
Alyssa. Her dishes are a big hit. There is
plenty of bannock (Inuit fried bread), and
a prized delicacy, raw narwhal skin.

Recently, Alyssa has seen a wide range of weather. In the north the weather was below freezing. Ottawa has been sunny and mild. But this morning brings powerful wind gusts and rain showers. Alyssa heads to the University of Ottawa, where she is a political science major, with a minor in aboriginal studies. "I learn a lot about my traditions at school, so it helps me do my work at ITK." Today she wears a cool-weather parka. Alyssa proudly points out that her mother made the parka, complete with fox fur trim. She hurries to get out of the rain and to her next appointment.

WORK AND PLAY
Taking a break from her lectures by relaxing at Parliament Hill.

Children await Alyssa's visit at the Ottawa Inuit Child Care Centre. Alyssa joins the children in daily rituals. Traditional songs, dancing, and language lessons bring a smile to Alyssa's face as she practices the customs of her heritage. The time goes quickly, but before she goes she joins in a friendly game of "throat singing." Women sing harsh melodic tones back and forth until one of them loses the rhythm. Alyssa loses the match, and almost loses her voice.

INUIT CULTURE
Alyssa helps children at the Ottawa Inuit Child Care Centre to learn about their heritage.

INUIT DOLL
Inuit children play with dolls dressed in traditional clothing.

At the end of the workday Alyssa heads to her family's home in the countryside in Almonte, Ontario. After soccer practice with her local women's team, Alyssa goes to her parents' house where she shares a video of her Iqaluit trip with her mother, Martha. Martha's face lights up at the glow of her family's campfire. "I am going up there in a few days, I can't wait," says Martha. They spend some precious minutes together and smile, united by the sights of their icy homeland. For this young Inuit woman there is a lot to smile about.

For this young Inuit woman there is a lot to smile about.

BALL CONTROL
Playing soccer with the local women's team is a fun way to keep healthy.

MOTHER AND DAUGHTER
Alyssa with her mother, Martha, at her family home.

FUR PARKA
Alyssa's mother made her a cool weather parka with a fox-fur trim.

Carolina *Mexico*

Carolina is a young woman from Mexico's state of Tamaulipas. She values her native culture and hopes for a better future.

During the week, Carolina rises early every day as breakfast is served promptly at 6:30 A.M. Carolina attends Technical High School #1 in Solis, Mexico. She shares a room in a boarding house with three other girls. It hasn't been easy. Carolina's family could not pay for her to attend the school, but through hard work she was able get a scholarship that made it possible. Carolina will be the first in her family to finish her high school and preparatory school studies. "I have seen how my sisters who did not study live, and I do not want that type of life for myself," she says.

HIGH SCHOOL
Technical High school #1, where Carolina studies, is located next to a pretty church in Solis.

CLASSMATES
Carolina gets along well with her school friends, and they help each other with their homework.

After school Carolina works in the school's computer lab until 6 P.M. and then attends a study session until 8 P.M. After dinner at 8 P.M., there is time to spend with her three roommates, or finish up any homework that still needs to be done. "We are supposed to be in bed by 10 P.M." Carolina laughs, "but often we are still awake when they come by at 11 P.M. to check on us and turn off the lights."

LOGGED ON
All pupils at Carolina's school have their own laptops.

> "I have seen how my sisters who did not study live, and I do not want that type of life for myself."
> *Carolina*

HELPING HAND
On weekends, Carolina helps her father bale hay at the family's farm.

Carolina knows if she wants to go to a university and get a degree she has to get good grades in school and get another scholarship. Carolina hopes to study medicine or communications in college. "Among my family and in my community there aren't too many professionals," Carolina admits. "That is what I wish for the most...to get my diploma and to have a better future."

Each weekend Carolina travels by bus for three hours back to her hometown. Along the way, she talks about how very different her life is at home. "San Nicolas de Guadalupe is a farming community full of hayfields and animals and plenty of dirt and dust," she says.

HOMETOWN
San Nicolas de Guadalupe, where Carolina's family live, is a small town at the heart of the farming community.

Fortunately, there are many other things that Carolina loves about her home. "The people there are very friendly," Carolina says. "When we have celebrations, everyone helps with the preparation of food and other things that need to be done."

Carolina, like most of the people in her hometown, is one of the Mazahua, an indigenous group. Carolina can speak her native language in addition to Spanish, but many young people cannot. "I have cousins and if I speak to them in Mazahua, they sit there thinking, 'What did she say?' They say that they should not speak Mazahua,

FLOWER POWER
An indigenous woman adorns her hat with colorful flowers for a celebration.

AT HOME
Carolina shares a relaxed meal with her brother and sister in the kitchen.

BREAD BASKET
A clay table and roller are used in making tortillas.

CYBER CAFÉ
Carolina spends a lot of time at her local Internet café, doing online research for her essays.

because they will not be accepted at school or because speaking Mazahua is something bad." Carolina is very concerned that if her people's native language is lost it will not be long before her entire culture vanishes. "So much is already being lost. Only the older women still dress in the traditional way."

It is already dark by the time Carolina steps off the bus in San Nicolas de Guadalupe and there is little left to do but have dinner and head off to bed for some much-deserved rest.

FAMILY PHOTO
Carolina's family at home in
San Nicolas de Guadalupe.

Tomorrow morning as Carolina
boards the bus back to school,
she won't be leaving
this all behind...she'll be
taking it with her
into the future.

TRADITIONAL CRAFTS
Carolina and her mother like
to do embroidery.

Carolina's weekends at home are spent doing household chores or helping in the fields, but usually she finds some time for fun. One of her favorite activities is riding her bike. She also likes to do traditional Mazahua crafts such as embroidery and knitting. Then, of course, there are Mazahua festivals. "I like to dance," Carolina says. "The *cumbia* (a dance from Colombia) and the *quebradita*, which is a Mexican version of the cumbia—at my house we dance to everything!"

As the music plays in the background and the sun sets on another weekend in San Nicolas de Guadalupe, Carolina finally gets a chance to sit back and enjoy the moment. Tomorrow morning as she boards the bus back to school, she won't be leaving this all behind...she'll be taking it with her into the future.

Luis *Dominican Republic*

This story features Luis, a teenager who lives in the Dominican Republic, one of the Caribbean islands. Luis is ambitious and hardworking, and wants eventually to leave his rural life and work in the city.

Luis's day usually begins with some chores around his house, a quick breakfast, and a bike ride to work. Luis lives in the rural town of Limón in the Dominican Republic. Limón is located on the Samaná Peninsula a few hours north of the Dominican Republic's capital city, Santo Domingo. The peninsula has white sandy beaches and lush tropical forests. It is home to a number of beautiful waterfalls. Perhaps the most spectacular waterfall in the region is Salto de Limón, which drops 150 feet into a deep pool of water. "A lot of tourists come to this area," Luis says, "and nearly all of them want to see the falls."

LUIS'S BIKE
Luis likes to go bike-riding when he has finished his chores.

TOURIST TRUCK
Some tourists travel by truck to the trail that leads to the falls.

Luis knows about tourists—he works as a tour guide leading visitors to Salto de Limón. The tourists usually ride horses on the journey, while Luis walks on foot to guide them.

Walking with tourists to a waterfall may sound like a simple job, but it is not. Visitors to the falls must climb up a steep trail for more than an hour to reach Salto de Limón. It can be a dangerous hike during the rainy season, when the trail is wet and slippery. But Luis has made this trip more than 200 times, and he knows the way well. When he was a child, he and his friends came here to swim and hunt for fresh fruit. Now Luis is almost 17 years old, and he enjoys taking tourists to this special place.

"A lot of tourists come to this area, and nearly all of them want to see the falls."

Luis

SPECTACULAR FALLS
Salto de Limón drops 150 feet into a deep pool of water.

TOURIST GUIDE
Luis guides tourists on horseback to the falls.

The natural beauty of the Samaná Peninsula makes it very popular with tourists. As a result, the government and the region's people are working to protect the waterfalls and the surrounding area. A local group of tourism-based businesses helps encourage the protection of natural resources and the environment.

SADDLING UP
Luis gets a horse ready for tourists to ride.

SUCCULENT PLANT
Colorful plants grow wild in the hot climate.

In Limón, Luis lives with his grandmother, Doña Graciela, and a few brothers and cousins. "My mother has been in Puerto Rico for eight years and my uncle lives in New York," he says. "My grandmother raised me."

Luis thinks of himself as an ordinary teenager. He begins a typical day by doing housework and shopping for groceries. "After my chores I like to go bike-riding," Luis says with a smile. He usually rides the mile or so to work, where he meets tourists ready to travel to Salto de Limón.

LUIS'S GRANDMOTHER PREPARING FOOD
Luis's grandmother, Doña Graciela, cooks for the whole family.

FAMILY MEAL
Luis and his family enjoy a meal together in the evenings.

LUIS IN CLASS
Attending school is important to Luis.

When Luis returns from leading a tour group to the falls, he is hot, tired, and often covered with mud. Then he gets ready to go to school in the afternoon. Not all Dominican children his age attend school, but Luis thinks it is important. "I want to finish my studies and get my worker's permit so I can work in the city," he says. Getting a work permit would lead to many opportunities for Luis. He wants to earn enough money to provide for his family, and he would love to be able to visit his mother in Puerto Rico.

Because it is not always tourist season in Limón, Luis also does *chiripeos*, or side jobs around town. Sometimes he works at construction sites. At harvest time, he helps the owner of a small organic coffee plantation pick and dry coffee beans. And, he adds, "Sometimes I go with my cousin to help with his grandmother's *conuco*." A conuco is a small plantation where families grow crops for their own use. Luis helps take care of the crops. Sometimes there are crops left over to sell, and Luis is able to make extra money.

BANANA CAFÉ
A small café sells coffee, cocoa, and water at the coffee plantation where Luis works.

COFFEE BEANS
Luis helps pick and dry coffee beans on a small coffee plantation.

No matter where you find Luis, one thing is clear: he is an extremely hardworking young man with a very bright future.

LUIS'S COUSINS
Some of Luis's cousins live with him and his grandmother.

Daniella *Colombia*

Daniella works as a tour guide on El Carriel, her family's coffee plantation in Colombia. She enjoys her job and the people she meets, but she hopes to be a cardiologist one day.

The quiet that blankets the lush green mountains is suddenly broken by the sound of an old pickup truck starting up. Daniella, a lively 15-year-old from the coffee region of Colombia, rushes to the vehicle. She has just finished her weekend work as a tour guide on her family's farm. Now she and her grandfather are about to drive into town. It is the harvest season and the pair are off to Quimbaya to sell part of this year's coffee crop.

COFFEE BEANS
Coffee beans from Daniella's plantation will be sold in Quimbaya in Quindio, Colombia.

SELLING TRIP
Daniella and her grandfather go to Quimbaya to sell their coffee crop.

COFFEE PLANTATION
Daniella's family home sits in the middle of their plantation.

"The farm has always been for growing coffee, and not only coffee, but other crops like plantain and beans, too."
Daniella

TOUR GUIDE
Daniella shows visitors a coffee plant on a tour of the farm.

The drive into town is short, and the scenery changes quickly. The soils in this part of Colombia are volcanic, which means the ground is very rich and fertile. Plantations and farms cover the hillsides. Closer to town, the plantations dotting the hills and valleys give way to one-family houses. Soon Daniella and her grandfather have arrived in the small but bustling downtown area, and the Plaza Bolívar—the square that is the central feature of almost every Colombian town and village.

While in Quimbaya, Daniella draws our attention to the tourists who have brought change to her region of Colombia.

COFFEE CHERRIES
The ripening fruits of the coffee tree are known as coffee cherries.

"The farm has always been for growing coffee, and not only coffee, but other crops like plantain and beans, too," explains Daniella. "But it isn't as easy as it used to be…. Then tourists started to come, and most locals thought that they could help us out economically and that we could enjoy each other as well."

Over the past two years El Carriel has undergone some changes. Handed down from her grandfather to her father, the coffee farm has expanded its activities to include tourism. New cabins have been built for the visitors. Her family is even planning to build a canopy line that will carry visitors through the treetops for a bird's-eye view of the farm and its surroundings.

TROPICAL PLANT
Exotic plants like heliconia grow in moist, warm clima[...]

PREPARING FOR A TOUR
Daniella waits at the farm with a basket of beans to use in a demonstration for her tour group.

TOURIST ATTRACTION
Visitors arrive at the farm on the back of a jeep.

During the week, Daniella lives in Armenia, where she goes to school. On weekends she travels from her home to work on the farm (near Quimbaya) as a tour guide. Here she educates tourists about the coffee process and daily life on the farm. Daniella enjoys the people who come to learn about her region, even though sometimes these foreigners can be difficult to understand. She explains that "Sometimes it gets complicated due to the language difference…. But we always try to learn from one another."

MOVING HOUSE
Over-laden jeeps like this toy are a common sight in Colombia.

Once in the marketplace, Daniella and her grandfather open their filled coffee sacks and have the beans tested for weight and quality. Then Daniella and her grandfather consult with the merchant over the price. After a little friendly haggling, all agree and set an amount. When paid, Daniella enjoys a quick game of bowling in the Quimbaya bowling alley. Then it's back to El Carriel.

Although she hopes to become a cardiologist one day, Daniella would still like to keep the farm in the family.

QUALITY CONTROL
During a visit to Quimbaya, a sample of beans is tested for quality to help determine a price.

On the farm, the heat of the afternoon gives way to a starry, early evening sky. The family all drink their last cup of coffee for the day as they chat. Daniella talks about her plans for the future. Although she hopes to become a cardiologist one day, she would still like to keep the farm in the family. Clearly enjoying the coffee produced here, she also explains why she enjoys the visitors, "We have conversations where we can learn about each other…besides making friends, I learn how they see things and then understand more about myself."

FAMILY TIME
When the tourists have gone, Daniella enjoys a cup of coffee with her mother and father.

LEISURE
After her work is done in Quimbaya, Daniella fits in some bowling before returning home.

Omar *Bolivia*

Omar is a young man who works under a mountain that once made an empire rich. He struggles to earn a living as a miner in Bolivia, but every day Omar goes to school and dreams of a better future.

Most days Omar follows the same routine: rising early, making his bed, eating breakfast, and heading off to work. He is only 14 years old but, like his father and grandfather before him, Omar is a miner. Six days a week Omar digs ore in the Paylaviri mine in Potosí, Bolivia. It's a typical story around here. Three of Omar's brothers are miners; so is his cousin, Frederico. In fact, almost all the men Omar knows have been miners at one time or another. Mining has a long and terrible history in this part of Bolivia, and Omar and Frederico must work under the mountain with the longest and most terrible mining history of them all—Cerro Rico, the "Rich Mountain."

TOOLS OF THE TRADE
A mallet and a flashlight are essential tools for miners.

DANGEROUS WORK
Working in the hot, dusty mine is very tiring and dangerous for boys like Omar and Frederico.

26

At 15,827 feet, Cerro Rico towers over the town of Potosí like a pyramid. For more than 450 years, generations of miners have dug into this mountain to extract its incredible wealth of silver and tin.

The locals say that so many tunnels have been carved into Cerro Rico that the mountain's heart is like Swiss cheese. The mine was discovered in 1544, and by 1600 it was producing half the world's silver, much of it sent to the Spanish king. But all that wealth came at a very high cost. More than 8 million people may have died here, either from mining accidents or as a result of illnesses caused by working underground. Omar knows this all too well. His own father became sick from breathing dust in the mine and died when Omar was ten.

PAYING RESPECTS
Whenever he visits his father's grave, Omar always brings a gift of flowers.

"Every time I go into the mine
I think it is the last time."
Omar

"I hate going down into the mine," Omar says. "Every time I go into the mine I think it is the last time. I think I won't be coming out." Fortunately, working conditions are better today than they were years ago. The miners have formed a cooperative. They work together to make conditions safer.

MINERS' STORE
Omar examines mining gear outside a store in Potosí.

Omar has to work for only a few hours each day, but those few hours are far from easy. "The work inside the mine is very tough. I have to run back and forth to dig ore. I also help my brothers or my cousin, Frederico, push the ore cart. It is very hot down underground. I have to carry enough water so I don't get thirsty. You sweat a lot in the mine. It is very difficult work. You have to dig very hard and sometimes it is dangerous, especially when you have to use dynamite."

PUSHING THE ORE CART
Both Omar and his cousin have to push metal carts in and out of the mine.

CHICKEN STEW
Every miner looks forward to a steaming bowl of traditional Bolivian stew.

A HEARTY MEAL
Omar and Frederico are hungry after their long working day.

After his father died, Omar's mother had to move away to find work. Working in the mine is the only way Omar and his brothers can make enough money to survive. "I make 250 Bolivianos, which is about 30 dollars per week. That's when I am lucky. Sometimes I only make 100 Bolivianos. . . . I give my brother some of that money to buy food for the house and sometimes I buy clothes. I also send my mother money to help raise my little brother."

FAMILY EXPECTATIONS
These young boys may have to work in the mine as soon as they are old enough.

Omar dreams that one day soon his life will change. He goes to school each afternoon after his shift at the mine. "I would like to become an architect when I grow up," he says. "I would like to build schools so other children all over the world can go to school too."

HIGH LIFE
Llamas live in the inhospitable landscape around Potosí.

FRESH PRODUCE
Omar and Frederico choose some bananas
on sale in the back of a truck.

BASKET OF FRUIT
A variety of different fruits
is sold in the market.

Working in the mine
is the only way Omar
and his brothers can
make enough money
to survive.

Despite all the hard work, Omar
still finds time to have fun. On this
day, he and Frederico stop by
a soccer court to join a game.
Frederico tackles the ball and
moves it quickly down the
court. Without even looking
up, he switches direction and
passes the ball to Omar on the
wing. Omar makes a move back
to the inside and drives the ball
past the goalkeeper. For now
Omar and Frederico are just
two happy cousins celebrating a
goal in the sun. Yet behind them
looms the peak of Cerro Rico,
reminding them that tomorrow
morning they will be under the
mountain once more.

TEAM PLAYERS
The local boys are proud
of their soccer team, and
they love to play hard after
working hard all day.

Vinicius *Brazil*

Vinicius is a 16-year-old soccer player who attends a training facility near Rio de Janeiro, Brazil. He hopes that one day he will be a professional and that success in sports will lead to a better life for him and his family.

It's a loud and thrilling Sunday afternoon at Maracanã Stadium in Rio de Janeiro, Brazil. Maracanã is the biggest soccer stadium in South America, and forty thousand fans are cheering for Flamengo, the most popular team in Brazil.

Flamengo is ahead by three goals, and the crowd has gone wild. The team's supporters are cheering, singing, and dancing to the traditional beats of the Brazilian samba. Dressed in their team's colors, they fill the stands with a loud and rippling sea of red and black.

But in the midst of all this excitement, one 16-year-old Flamengo supporter stays quiet. Vinicius is too busy studying the players' techniques. That's because for Vinicius soccer is not just a game—it's a passport to a better life for him and his family.

TEAM'S COLORS
Flamengo supporters wear black and red stripes, the team's colors.

YOUTH TEAM
The young players take a break from training to listen to their sports coaches.

Two years ago, Vinicius was selected from thousands of young hopefuls to play for Flamengo's youth division. This was the first step in a process that might lead to a professional contract. Playing for the Flamengo team could make Vinicius a star.

Vinicius says, "It's so exciting to come to the stadium and see the professionals on the field, because I hope that will be me in the future, playing for a huge cheering crowd shouting my name. It is my ultimate dream!"

"It's so exciting to come to the stadium and see the professionals on the field, because I hope that will be me in the future."
Vinicius

TACKLING PRACTICE
The youth team practices their tackling techniques.

The next day, the whistle blows at the Flamengo training facility near Rio. Forty boys aged 14 to 17 dressed in red and black uniforms are running drills with a coach. Vinicius, the only player with a Mohawk hairstyle, is there, taking up his position as a forward on the team.

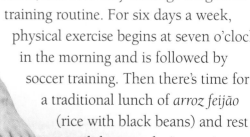

TAKING A PASS
Vinicius anticipates a pass from one of his team players.

These boys were selected from all over Brazil, and here they undergo a rigorous training routine. For six days a week, physical exercise begins at seven o'clock in the morning and is followed by soccer training. Then there's time for a traditional lunch of *arroz feijão* (rice with black beans) and rest until the next day's practice.

TRAINING SCHEDULE
Vinicius follows a rigorous training schedule six days a week.

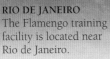

RIO DE JANEIRO
The Flamengo training
facility is located near
Rio de Janeiro.

VINICIUS WITH HIS PARENTS
Vinicius's family lives in Belém,
in the Amazon rain forest.

Brazil is a country with widespread poverty and a huge gap between rich and poor. For young people from poorer families, success at sports is one of the few ways to achieve a more comfortable life.

For now, Rio will be his home as he waits to find out whether he will advance to the next level of the Flamengo youth team. Rio is world famous for its beaches and tourist attractions, but Vinicius doesn't get much time to see the sights. When he's not busy training, he goes to night classes to complete his high school diploma so he can enter a university.

For Vinicius, pursuing his dream has meant sacrifice. He moved far from his hometown of Belém, more than 1,500 miles north of Rio de Janeiro. Belém is located in the huge Amazon rain forest. He left behind his mother, who works as a secretary, and his father, a math teacher.

Vinicius loves the rain forest and regrets its ongoing destruction. "There are many green areas, trees, and rivers. But people are destroying it. There are trees that are over a hundred years old, but people are cutting the trees for wood and also polluting the rivers."

His new life away from home has not been easy. In the southeastern city of Rio de Janeiro, Vinicius has faced prejudice against people from the North, which is a poor region. "Some people called me names when I first arrived. It was upsetting," he explains. "And I really miss my family. I have cried several times, but I remember that I am here hoping to give them a better life."

TOURIST HOT SPOTS
Vinicius relaxes on
Rio de Janeiro's famous
Copacabana beach.

32

FREE TIME
When he is not training, Vinicius likes
to stroll along the water front.

"Some players do sign a professional
contract, but there are those who
don't succeed, or who get injured, so
I think it is important to have a 'Plan
B.' I am thinking of studying physical
education at university," he says.

ONE STEP CLOSER
Vinicius is given a place on the
youth team for another year.

Back on the soccer field, the head coach announces the
selections for the following year. Some of the boys put on a
brave face when they discover they haven't made the list.

But Vinicius has a big smile. Although he has not been
offered a professional contract, he's been invited back for
another year on the youth team and is one step closer to his
dream. "If I become professional one day, it will be worth all
of this sacrifice of being far from home," he grins.

ALTERNATIVE PLAN
If he doesn't become a professonal player,
Vinicius might study physical education.

PICKED FOR THE TEAM
Everyone on the youth team hopes to
play professionally one day.

"If I become
professional one day,
it will be worth all of
this sacrifice of being
far from home."
Vinicius

Yasmin *Sweden*

This story features Yasmin, a young woman who was born in Madrid but lives in Sweden. She has family in Spain and Pakistan.

Yasmin straps on her dancing shoes. She glances in the mirror, adjusts her dress, and taps her way into the dance studio. With a rose in her hair and a colorful shawl stretched between her hands, Yasmin practices *flamenco*, a traditional Spanish dance. Inside the studio, the music makes Yasmin think of the warm Mediterranean while Sweden's winter winds blow outside.

Yasmin was born in Madrid, Spain, but she lives with her family in the coastal town of Bjärred in southern Sweden. Her father, Asif, is Pakistani and Spanish. Her mother, Monica, is Finnish and Swedish. Yasmin took both of her parents' names as a tribute to her heritage.

Asif left Spain to work in Sweden in 1995. At that time, Sweden had just become a member of the European Union (EU). EU member countries allow people to move across borders without passports or complicated documents. Asif decided to try life in Sweden, where more jobs were available. So, at age six Yasmin, along with her sister, Sabina, and brother, Daniel, moved to frosty Sweden—a completely different world from Spain.

YASMIN WITH HER PARENTS
Yasmin's father is Pakistani and Spanish, and her mother is Finnish and Swedish.

Yasmin remembers that she wasn't ready for the change in cultures. "At first, I was very different from the Swedish girls. In general, Swedes are much more quiet than Spaniards. I spoke very loud…I was a Spanish girl, and I yelled and ran around everywhere. I was more like the Swedish boys."

FARMERS' MARKET
Fresh seasonal vegetables are available at the open-air market.

STARK CONTRAST
When her family moved from Spain to Sweden, Yasmin had to get used to a different climate.

At home, Yasmin speaks Spanish with her father and Swedish with her mother. Everyone also speaks English. "The language that we speak is similar to the foods we eat. It is very mixed up," laughs Yasmin. She adds, "Sometimes we mix up our languages, even though our parents say we shouldn't. It's just easier to find the word you are looking for in another language. We even mix up languages within one sentence—but we all understand each other."

"The language that we speak is similar to the foods we eat. It is very mixed up."
Yasmin

THE TOWN OF LUND
Yasmin rides the bus from Bjärred to Lund to attend the university.

Even the family meal is a cultural medley. "We make it up as we go," explains Asif as he dices potatoes. He is making a Pakistani dish called *alu gosht*, a sort of a beef stew. Yasmin explains that this alu gosht includes Spanish olive oil, Swedish potatoes, and Chinese rice. The olive oil comes from the family's own olive trees in Spain!

SWEDISH MEATBALLS
Meatballs are a favorite Swedish dish.

LUND CATHEDRAL
Yasmin in front of Lund's medieval cathedral.

One of Yasmin's favorite possessions is her video camera. She has made several videos, including many that documented her trip to meet family in Pakistan. Music is also important to Yasmin, and she can play the piano, the flute, and the guitar.

Most days, Yasmin rides the bus to Lund to attend university classes. Lund is a medieval city full of gothic architecture and winding streets. Higher education is free in Sweden, so students from all over the world come to Lund University. Yasmin has many interests such as film and architecture, but she hasn't decided on a major.

AT THE PIANO
Yasmin plays several musical instruments including the piano.

One of Yasmin's new hobbies is tae kwon do, a form of martial arts that developed in Korea. At a *dojo* (a martial arts training school) near the university, she puts on a white uniform and her blue belt. Barefoot, Yasmin and a partner practice a complex routine designed for self-defense.

"Tae kwon do has a philosophy of peace," Yasmin says, "that teaches me to have the right mindset in order to be able to do the sport correctly."

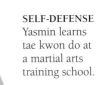

AT LUND UNIVERSITY
Yasmin attends class at Lund University, popular with students from all over the world.

Whether she's ice-skating, studying, or making a video, Yasmin has many choices, since Europe is at her doorstep.

SELF-DEFENSE
Yasmin learns tae kwon do at a martial arts training school.

Back in Bjärred, Yasmin walks along the beach. It's cold and windy, but beautiful. Bjärred is famous for its 500-meter pier into the strait of Öresund. It is the longest pier in the country. At the end of the pier is the Bjärred Kallbadhus (bathhouse). In the winter, people dive from the sauna there into the icy waters of the Öresund. Walking over the snow-covered dunes, Yasmin thinks about how much she cherishes the blazing sun of Spain. At the same time, she looks forward to ice-skating near her home in Sweden. Whether she's ice-skating, studying, or making a video, Yasmin has many choices, since Europe is at her doorstep.

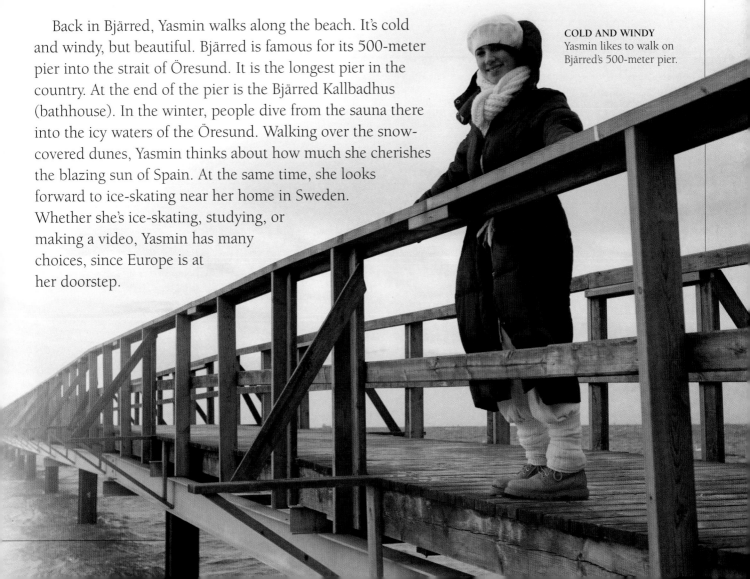

COLD AND WINDY
Yasmin likes to walk on Bjärred's 500-meter pier.

Serhiy *Ukraine*

Serhiy lives in a small village in Ukraine. Like all young people who live there, Serhiy will have to leave the village for work when he graduates.

Serhiy lives in the historic farming hamlet of Bezpalche, located 80 miles (130 kilometers) east of the Ukrainian capital of Kiev. Its 640 people are proud of the village's roots. It was founded by Bezpalko, a famous Cossack. The Cossacks were free-roaming bands of warriors known for their expert horsemanship and fierce fighting tactics. They defended the Ukrainian frontiers from enemy attack.

Single-family brick homes with tile roofs line the village lanes. Wooden fences separate the yards. Behind the houses are small plots of land used for farming. A wooden Christian church is the tallest structure in the village. A village school stands in the center of the village along an unpaved road. The village is small enough that it is easy to get around by walking.

WALKING TO SCHOOL
Serhiy walks to school along an unpaved road.

SCHOOL BUILDING
Serhiy attends the village school where he is in his final year.

CHICKEN RUN
Chickens and geese run around
outside the small farm where
Serhiy lives with his family.

This school is where 16-year-old Serhiy enjoys his favorite subjects of physical education, information technology, and the Ukrainian language. In his final year of study, Serhiy walks to school from home, where he lives with his parents, his older brother, and his elderly grandmother.

His mother works a postal route three hours a day. On their small farm, his family grows beets, onions, cabbage, corn, and potatoes, and tends four pigs and three milking cows. Serhiy is personally responsible for caring for more than 40 rabbits. Small farms like this are common in Ukraine.

DRYING CORN
Serhiy's family grows corn
and other vegetables.

FEEDING TIME
Serhiy tends
the family's
pigs.

At sunset, Serhiy starts his homework.

GRINDING CORN
Dried corn is
ground by hand
for chicken feed.

Ukraine used to be part of the Soviet Union. The Soviet government managed all the land in the country. Now Ukraine is an independent country. The new leadership broke up the large government farms, giving each family a small plot of land.

In villages like these, nature doesn't allow for breaks or long vacations. Serhiy rises at 6:00 A.M., feeds the livestock, and does other chores around the pens. Then he eats breakfast and heads to school for his first class, which begins at 8:30. He returns home at 2:30 P.M. and eats lunch. His favorite lunch is potatoes fried in lard and onions. His next chore is to take care of the rabbits. His grandmother pays him a small weekly allowance for this task. Then, at sunset, Serhiy starts his homework.

Short and broad-shouldered, Serhiy enjoys physical activity. He loves motorbikes and anything technical. "I even assembled a computer from scratch with a friend of mine," Serhiy says proudly, pointing at his PC, which he knows inside and out.

But Serhiy can enjoy these hobbies only when time permits. On the weekends, his brother drives him 25 miles (40 kilometers) to the regional capital to take preparatory classes. Serhiy wants to go to the military academy in Kharkiv in eastern Ukraine. He hopes to become a pilot. But to do so, he will need to do well on the entrance exam. The prestigious and highly competitive academy accepts only one out of every four applicants.

COMPUTER GAMES
The village has no Internet access, but Serhiy plays games on a computer that he assembled from scratch.

GROCERY STORE
Serhiy buys bread at the village shop.

Serhiy knows his small world and way of life will come to an end next summer when he graduates. Even if he is not accepted to the military academy, he will leave his village. The grocery store is the only real business in Bezpalche, so most young people must go elsewhere to make a living. Once his studies begin, he will not be able to take trips into the woods or drive his motorbike on country roads.

LOCAL TRANSPORT
Many people in the village travel by horse and cart.

GOOD FRIENDS
Like all young people his ...
chat with friends aft...

"No one ... in the village next summer ... in the village

Still, Serhiy looks forward to military life. After all, could it be tougher than life in Bezpalche? Yet he worries, "Cities have wide boulevards, and I'll be a stranger among impersonal strangers."

He's willing to make the transition since he is drawn to the physical rigor of military exercises, the technical hardware and weaponry, and the challenges the regimen brings. "My family supports my decision, and my mother just worries like any other mother does," Serhiy says half-jokingly.

KIEV MARKET
The city of Kiev is about 80 miles from Serhiy's village.

"My family supports my decision, and my mother just worries like any other mother does."
Serhiy

FUTURE PLANS
If he doesn't get into the military academy, Serhiy plans to study computer programming.

HOMEWORK
After he has finished his farm chores, Serhiy begins his homework.

And if he doesn't get accepted when he applies in Kharkiv next summer, what is his backup plan? "Then I'll probably study computer programming in Cherkassy, the neighboring regional capital," Serhiy says.

How does he feel about leaving an environment where everything is familiar, where there are no surprises, and where everybody knows his name? "Well, I'm not just going to stay here," he says. "No one from my graduating class plans to remain in the village next summer, nobody."

Boris *Russia*

Boris lives in Moscow, which is the largest city in Russia. He loves skateboarding and travels the world to participate in competitions.

It's a sunny day in Moscow, and people hurry past a huge monument to the German philosopher Karl Marx. The 200-ton block of stone bears the inscription "Workers of the world, unite," a quote from Marx that became famous among communist workers. When the statue was unveiled in 1961, Russia was a communist nation, and Marx was an honored figure.

Today, Russia is a very different place, and the monument to Marx is better known as a fun place for skateboarders to try tricks like the ollie or the bigspin.

SKATEBOARD JUMPS
Boris practices tricks on his skateboard.

GOOD FRIENDS
Like all young people his age, Boris likes to chat with friends after school.

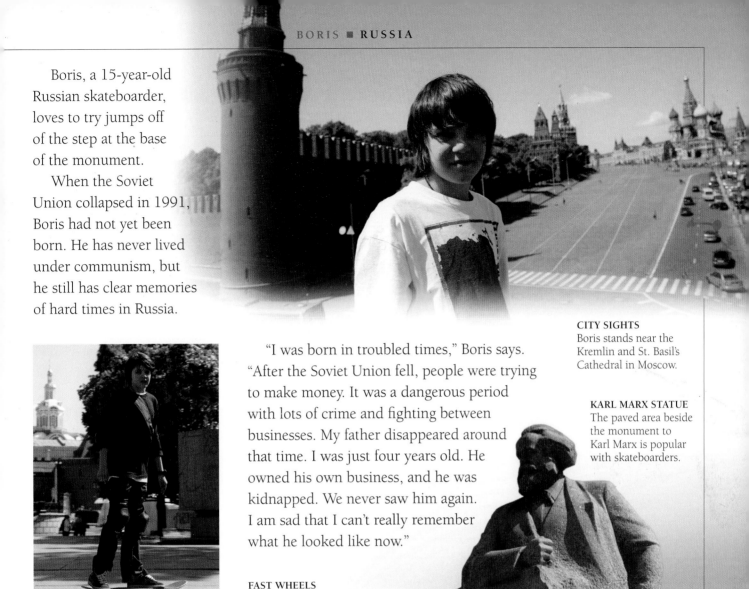

Boris, a 15-year-old Russian skateboarder, loves to try jumps off of the step at the base of the monument.

When the Soviet Union collapsed in 1991, Boris had not yet been born. He has never lived under communism, but he still has clear memories of hard times in Russia.

"I was born in troubled times," Boris says. "After the Soviet Union fell, people were trying to make money. It was a dangerous period with lots of crime and fighting between businesses. My father disappeared around that time. I was just four years old. He owned his own business, and he was kidnapped. We never saw him again. I am sad that I can't really remember what he looked like now."

CITY SIGHTS
Boris stands near the Kremlin and St. Basil's Cathedral in Moscow.

KARL MARX STATUE
The paved area beside the monument to Karl Marx is popular with skateboarders.

FAST WHEELS
Boris travels around Moscow by skateboard.

"It was a dangerous period with lots of crime and fighting between businesses. My father disappeared around that time."
Boris

Boris goes everywhere by skateboard, including the skate park. At the indoor skate park, curved ramps are everywhere, and the clatter of decks hitting the floor fills the air.

During the Soviet era, the sport of skateboarding did not exist. Boris is one of the first young Russians to take part in paid skateboard competitions. He even has a sponsorship by a major sports brand—something else that's new in Russia.

"There was no skateboarding during Soviet times—things have changed so much since then. In those days, people couldn't travel at all outside the Soviet Union. Today, I am able to travel all over the world to participate in competitions."

HITTING AIR
Boris loves to try jumps off the steps around Moscow's public plazas.

SKATE PARK
The indoor skate park, which did not exist during the Soviet era, is a great place to practice.

"My mom was really proud when I started winning competitions. She was amazed when I managed to get a sponsorship deal."

Boris

44

"My mom was really proud when I started winning competitions," Boris recalls. "She was amazed when I managed to get a sponsorship deal. It was a really nice moment for me when I could use some of my prize money to make her birthday special."

Boris says that his mother and stepfather are proud of his skateboarding, although they worry about him being injured. They also hope that he will consider a professional career someday. "Moscow is growing so quickly that I've become interested in real estate!" Boris laughs.

SLIP UP
Boris's mother and stepfather worry about the dangerous side of the sport.

AIMING HIGH
Boris likes playing basketball in the local park.

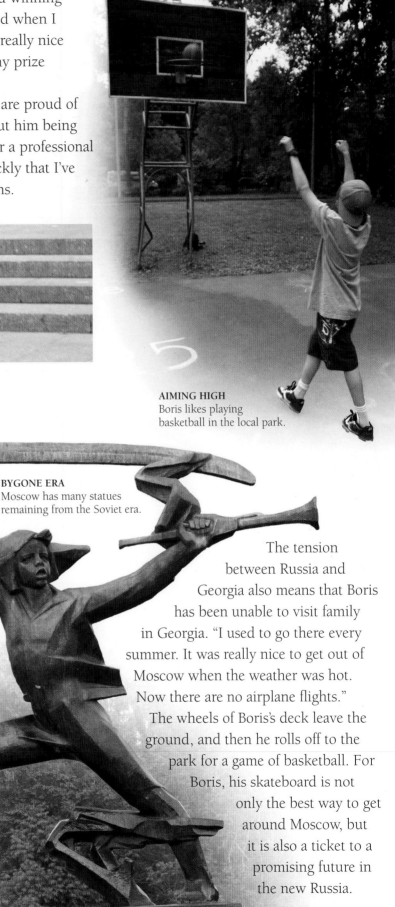

BYGONE ERA
Moscow has many statues remaining from the Soviet era.

Following the 2008 Russian invasion of Georgia, Boris decided to change his last name. Georgia had once been part of the Soviet Union, but it declared its independence in 1991. Since then, relations have been tense between Russia and Georgia.

"My father was half Georgian, and he had a very un-Russian sounding last name. With all the problems between our two countries, my mom decided that we should change our name. I was really sad because I felt like I was giving away a piece of my father, but really we had no choice. Russians have become quite anti-Georgian and my name marked me as different."

The tension between Russia and Georgia also means that Boris has been unable to visit family in Georgia. "I used to go there every summer. It was really nice to get out of Moscow when the weather was hot. Now there are no airplane flights." The wheels of Boris's deck leave the ground, and then he rolls off to the park for a game of basketball. For Boris, his skateboard is not only the best way to get around Moscow, but it is also a ticket to a promising future in the new Russia.

Evelyn *Ghana*

In this story, you'll read about Evelyn from Ghana in Africa who works in her grandmother's bead-making business but hopes to study accounting at a university.

The Kenashie Market in Accra, Ghana, is full of vendors selling everything from coconuts and chickens to textiles and furniture. Men, women, and children of all ages hustle to sell the goods balanced atop their heads or heaped in their heavy carts. In West Africa, where Ghana is located, there is a long tradition of women trading in the marketplace. In some countries, women organize and dominate many local markets. Overall, though, women earn less than men. In Ghana, only 70 percent of women can read and write, in contrast to 84 percent of men.

A BOWL OF BEADS
Ghanaian beads are renowned for their bright, colorful patterns.

LIVELY MARKET
Kenashie market in Accra is a colorful, bustling place where all types of goods and produce are sold.

Evelyn, a 15-year-old Ghanaian girl, takes part in her region's tradition of women selling goods in the marketplace. She helps her grandmother make and sell their authentic Ghanaian beads at different markets near their home village of Kpong. Kpong lies about 30 miles away from the bustling markets of Accra. Kpong is Evelyn's home and where her grandmother's bead business, Adede Beads Enterprises, is located. The plantain farms and thick greenery that surround the small village of Kpong are very different from Accra.

PLANTAIN TREE
Plantain farms surround Kpong, where Evelyn and her family live.

EYE-CATCHING SIGN
The sign for the family bead business is visible from the roadway.

BEAD-MAKING
Evelyn's grandmother looks on as Evelyn crushes bottle glass to make a fine powder that is then sifted into a bowl.

Evelyn's grandmother, Madam Adede, is a successful entrepreneur herself. She has been running the bead business she inherited from her grandfather for more than 31 years. Adede owns a humble home where she and her family live and work. The small building in the backyard serves as her bead factory.

"After university, I'll get a job outside and help my grandma, too, because I have my siblings to take care of."

Evelyn

Adede specializes in the ancient craft of bead making practiced by the Krobo people of eastern Ghana. Adede taught this craft to two daughters and six grandchildren. She expects the business to continue for many generations. Adede has chosen Evelyn to take over her business someday. Evelyn has just graduated from high school. She hopes to study accounting at a university. But the cost won't be easy for her family to afford.

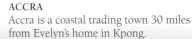

ACCRA
Accra is a coastal trading town 30 miles from Evelyn's home in Kpong.

Evelyn already plays an important role in the family business. It is her job to crush glass in preparation for making the beads. Today she is making transparent glass beads, which are formed from a very fine glass powder. Evelyn begins by breaking glass bottles they have collected. It is hard work, but Evelyn is accustomed to the heavy labor and stifling heat that comes with everyday life at the bead factory in Kpong.

FIRING KILN
The powdered glass is poured into molds and fired in a kiln to make the beads.

GLASS CRUSHING
Evelyn pounds the glass inside a pail, which protects her eyes from flying shards.

Crushing the glass is the first of many steps necessary to produce a finished piece of clear beaded jewelry. Adede explains that they also make glazed beads and *bodom* beads. The word bodom means "dog" in Twi, a common language in Ghana. The bodom beads are very large, bold beads, named for their resemblance to the attention-getting bark of a dog.

Beads, such as those made by Evelyn, are worn not only for adornment, but also to identify the various ethnic cultures of Ghana. Beads are often worn at parties, weddings, and church services.

NECKLACES
The women of the family thread the finished beads onto string to make necklaces.

BEAD STAND
Evelyn sells bead necklaces from a stand
in the front yard of their home.

Today the family is taking its beads to sell at the
Krobo Odumase Market a few miles from Kpong. Adede's
bead stand in the marketplace displays their colorful
jewelry to the buyers in the market. Everyone works hard
to sell as much as possible. They need money not only to
support the family but also to send Evelyn to a university.

For her part, Evelyn plans to pay back this kindness.
Evelyn says, "After university, I'll get a job outside and
help my grandma, too, because I have my siblings to take
care of. It's important to have two jobs. So if one fails, you
have the other one." The road ahead of Evelyn is difficult,
but her family's bead business has paved the way.

SOMETHING TO CELEBRATE
Family and friends express their
delight in being involved in a
thriving business.

MARKET TRADING
The beads made by Evelyn's
family are also sold at the
Krobo Odumase market.

The road ahead
of Evelyn is difficult, but
her family's bead business
has paved the way.

Khulekani *South Africa*

Khulekani is a young South African man who lives in Port Saint Johns. Life is hard, but Khulekani believes in his future and in the future of South Africa.

At 19, Khulekani is a young man with strong principles and big dreams. Khulekani is a member of the Xhosa (KOH sah) people, the second-largest ethnic group in South Africa. His parents passed away ten years ago. Now he lives with his aunt and his sister.

Khulekani lives in a settlement called Nonyevu, on a hill that overlooks the town of Port Saint Johns, in the Transkei region of South Africa. Behind the town is the mighty Umzimvubu River. From Khulekani's home, the view of the lush, tropical landscape is spectacular. Still, life can be difficult for Khulekani and his family.

NO WATER OR ELECTRICITY
For Khulekani, life can be hard because of the lack of facilities in his settlement.

BEAUTIFUL LANDSCAPE
The countryside around Port Saint Johns, where Khulekani lives, is spectacular and popular with tourists.

WATER CARRIER
Khulekani is responsible for collecting enough water every day for all his family's needs.

"We have no water or electricity in Nonyevu. This is a problem for me because I often get homework that requires me to watch television. Without electricity I cannot watch television. When my school shirt gets dirty and there is no rainwater I have to use water from the tap in town, and this water is not clean enough for washing."

Along with water and electricity, healthcare is also lacking in parts of Transkei. The HIV/AIDS epidemic has taken a heavy toll in this area.

Until 1994, the apartheid system oppressed black South Africans. Under apartheid, white South Africans controlled the country, even though black South Africans are a majority. Since the fall of apartheid, South Africans of all races have shared power. The racial divide is slowly healing. Like most young South Africans today Khulekani has moved past the racial divisions of the past.

"You see, now everything is right, because we are equal."
Khulekani

GOOD FRIENDS
It is important for Khulekani to find time in his busy day to see his friends.

DOING THE LAUNDRY
Clothes must be washed
by hand using rainwater.

"You see, now everything is right," he says, "because we are equal. White people can help black people if they are suffering. Black men have also oppressed other black men, so all in all, it just depends on how good or nice you are, rather than your skin color. Either way you are equal."

Still, like all South Africans, Khulekani is aware of the huge gap between developed and undeveloped areas in his country. He and his family struggle to get by, but many South Africans, mostly white, live more comfortable lives.

On a typical morning, Khulekani wakes up at 6 A.M. and boils water on his gas stove for a bath. He makes his breakfast, usually bread and tea. Then its time to go to school. Khulekani walks to school, where he is in eleventh grade. When he finishes school next year, he hopes to study at a nearby university. His goal is to graduate and become an accountant.

BREAKFAST
Khulekani
prepares
breakfast on
his gas stove.

SCHOOLWORK
Khulekani studies
hard at school because
he wants to go to
a university.

Having breakfast and rushing off to school are things teenagers do all over the world. But because Khulekani's family is so poor, everyday routines can be challenging. For example, just to have enough water for drinking, cooking, and washing, Khulekani must carry six-gallon jugs of water more than a half a mile. He is responsible for carrying all the water his family needs.

"You must not waste things like water and just throw them away. I don't have the means to get new things so I must look after what I have. The things we have must only be used in the right way in order to survive."

Despite the challenges he faces, Khulekani remains positive, "Yes, things like carrying water from town and doing homework without electricity can affect my schoolwork but I can work past those things."

CHOIR PRACTICE
Singing Xhosa hymns with the choir is the highlight of Khulekani's day.

BRIGHT FUTURE
Khulekani has a big smile because he is positive about the future.

> Khulekani believes that once he has made his own way in the world, he can come back and help fix the problems in his town.

Today, being involved at school helps Khulekani enjoy his life. He runs a local youth leadership group, for example. "I like to be involved with the youth group. I like to do positive things."

Khulekani is also a part of the school choir. He is optimistic about the choir. He tells us it is the highlight of his day. "The reason I want to sing in the choir is because I want to take advantage of my opportunities. I want to learn how to do everything in life."

They sing mostly Xhosa hymns, and Khulekani finds joy when he is singing with the choir. "I like to be happy, and singing with other kids makes me happy. It's very nice. It takes away the worries."

Khulekani believes in his future and the future of South Africa. He believes that once he has made his own way in the world, he can come back and help fix the problems in his town.

Shaimaa *Egypt*

This story features Shaimaa, a young Egyptian woman who lives in Cairo, the capital of Egypt. She is proud of her heritage and works hard to make younger people feel the same.

Sitting on the top of Cairo's medieval city wall, 18-year-old Shaimaa is focused on her sketchbook. Pencil in hand, she traces the domes and towers that make up the skyline of Darb al-Ahmar, the neighborhood where she was born and raised. Her spot overlooks a large park, and the sound of birds fills the air. For Shaimaa, it seems a million miles away from the hustle and bustle of the crowded neighborhood below where she lives with her family.

"I have four sisters. We all sleep in the same room. My older sister Asmaa got married. They had to leave the area because they couldn't afford an apartment."

CITY WALL
Shaimaa sketches the city skyline from high up on the medieval city wall.

SHAIMAA, HER MOTHER, AND ONE OF HER SISTERS
Shaimaa has four sisters but one has now left home because she is married.

Shaimaa's parents, like many in the neighborhood, moved here from the countryside. They originally came from a village in southern Egypt. They moved to Cairo to find a new life.

Shaimaa's apartment is located in one of the hundreds of small alleys that make up Darb al-Ahmar. The neighborhood lies in the shadow of the citadel, or fortress. The citadel was once home to Cairo's rulers and its wealthiest families lived in Darb al-Ahmar.

CITY SKYLINE
The panorama of Shaimaa's neighborhood includes the citadel and its alabaster mosque with twin minarets. This impressive building was built between 1830 and 1848.

"I have four sisters. We all sleep in the same room."
Shaimaa

DARB AL-AHMAR
Shaimaa lives in one of the many small alleys in Darb al-Ahmar, an old part of the city.

The neighborhood was very prosperous. Its wealthy residents built beautiful mosques. But later, the area fell on hard times. For many years the beautiful buildings crumbled. As the population mushroomed, the area became overcrowded. Like many parts of Cairo today, Shaimaa's neighborhood is struggling to support a growing population.

HIGH ABOVE THE CITY
From her vantage point on the city wall, Shaimaa can look down on the many restoration projects going on in her neighborhood.

Every weekday Shaimaa leaves her house at 9 A.M. and makes her way through the bustling market to catch a bus to school in downtown Cairo. She is studying computer science and hopes to continue at a university at the end of the year.

However, Shaimaa's real passion is to help restore her neighborhood. Most days after school she volunteers at a community center to do her part.

With hammer in hand, Shaimaa nails together a wooden backdrop, painted with the minarets and domes of Darb al-Ahmar's distinctive skyline. Today she is helping a group of children to prepare a puppet show on the history of their neighborhood. Puppet shows are a traditional form of entertainment. Shaimaa hopes that by bringing these old stories to life, she may be able to encourage a sense of pride in the neighborhood.

PUPPET
A traditional character from the puppet show

STREET MARKET
Shaimaa buys fruit at the local street market.

PUPPET SHOW
The history of the neighborhood is retold with the help of local children.

"We are trying to tell the people about this neighborhood through the program. We are trying to make people proud of Darb al-Ahmar by reminding them about their history, trying to revive the heritage and the folklore of the neighborhood."

In the courtyard of the school, the children rehearse the puppet show. In two weeks they will be performing it in the park by the city wall. It's hard to believe now, but the park was a garbage dump until a few years ago. After centuries of people throwing their trash over the wall, the dump grew into a hill, Shaima recalls.

"I remember before it was a park, it was a dusty hill. We were frightened to go in there because the wild dogs would chase us."

PUPPET SHOW BACKDROP
Shaimaa helped create this backdrop,
using the sights of Darb al-Ahmar for inspiration.

"I hope that I'll have more chances to represent the habits and traditions of my neighborhood and to let other people know more about Darb al-Ahmar."
Shaimaa

Sketching on the top of the wall, Shaimaa gazes down on her neighborhood. She points out the buildings that are undergoing restoration.

"Here, each house is like a piece of art from the past. After being restored, each house regains its sense of history."

Shaimaa is optimistic about the future of her neighborhood. "I hope that I'll have more chances to represent the habits and traditions of my neighborhood and to let other people know more about Darb al-Ahmar."

DEEP IN THOUGHT
Shaimaa concentrates on her sketches.

Hanan *Saudi Arabia*

Hanan is a young Saudi woman who has become a professional in a country where women face many difficulties. She looks forward to a long career as a nurse.

In the darkness of the early morning, Hanan awakes to the sound of *adhan*. This is the Islamic call to prayer, sung out by a *muezzin*, often from the minaret, or high tower, of an Islamic house of worship called a mosque. The adhan call tells the faithful that it is time to begin their daily prayer rituals. They will perform these rituals five times over the course of the day.

As the muezzin's voice drifts through the warm stillness remaining from the night, it is joined by another, then another, and yet another voice calling out the prayer, in Arabic: "*Allahu akbar. Hayya alal sala. Hayya alal falah.*" That is Arabic for "God is most great. Come to prayer. Come to success."

MORNING PRAYER
From minarets all over the city, the muezzin's voice calls the faithful to prayer.

STILLNESS
Hanan's neighborhood awakes from the warm stillness of the night.

URBAN LANDSCAPE
Hanan's family lives in the ancient city of Jidda,
now a modern metropolis.

"As Muslims, we pray five times a day. It is great to be able to take that break from everything and just focus on God."
Hanan

The calling continues as Hanan walks to the bathroom to make her *wudu*, her ritual washing before beginning prayer. She covers herself from head to toe with her *sharshaf*, a long, traditional robe, and joins her mother for the first prayer of the day.

FAMILY TIME
Hanan and her family relax in their living room.

AT PRAYER
Dressed in traditional robes, Hanan
and her mother pray together.

"As Muslims, we pray five times a day. It is great to be able to take that break from everything and just focus on God. Starting your day with *Salah* [prayer] gives your life purpose. You make your intention that everything you do that day is for God. That way all your deeds become a form of worship," says Hanan.

Hanan is 20 years old. Hanan lives in the city of Jidda in the Kingdom of Saudi Arabia. She lives with her parents, two brothers, and one sister.

Hanan has recently graduated from nursing school. She now works at Erfan hospital in Jidda. She has always been interested in medicine, but began focusing specifically on nursing after accompanying another nurse on the job one day.

Hanan says, "So many people ask me why I decided to be a nurse instead of a doctor. I love nursing! As a doctor you don't get to spend that much time with a patient. Doctors mostly diagnose and prescribe medicine. As nurses, we spend most of our time with patients. We are the ones who hold their hands when they are scared and stand beside them in their time of need. We are there for families as well as patients. Being able to help people and hear them praying for me surpasses all other feelings."

JOURNEY TO WORK
Every day, Hanan is driven to the hospital where she works.

Many nurses in Saudi Arabia come from other countries, but the number of Saudi nurses is growing. Nursing, however, is not a typical profession for Saudi women.

In fact, few Saudi women work outside the home. Saudi law and culture place many restrictions on the lives of women. For example, Saudi women are not legally allowed to drive cars. They may not travel abroad without the permission of their husband or a male relative.

Saudi culture strongly encourages women to stay home and take care of their families rather than work. Because of these cultural and legal restrictions it is difficult for them to hold jobs. Still, 5 percent of Saudi women work outside their homes.

AN ANCIENT CITY
Many buildings in Jidda have traditional Arab architecture.

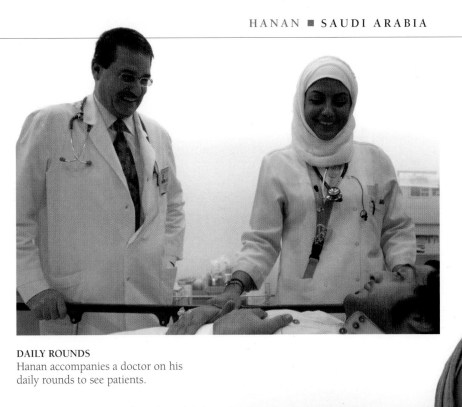

DAILY ROUNDS
Hanan accompanies a doctor on his
daily rounds to see patients.

Despite the hardships
she sometimes faces,
Hanan loves her job and
looks forward to a long
career in her chosen
field of nursing.

Restrictions aside, Hanan's biggest headache is her
hectic schedule. The necessity of working around-the-
clock in shifts takes a toll on family life.

"Nursing is a tough profession," Hanan says. "People
who want to go into this line of work need to have
patience and endurance. I end up missing a lot of family
gatherings due to long working hours. I sometimes stay
at home on my days off just to get some rest."

Despite the hardships she sometimes faces, Hanan
loves her job and looks forward to a long career
in her chosen field of nursing.

PREPARING DINNER
Her younger brother helps Hanan
to prepare the evening meal.

Maayan and Muhammad *Israel*

Life for Arab and Jewish Israelis is very different. Maayan, a young Jewish woman, will have to do military service, while Muhammad, an Arab boy, is kept out of the West Bank by a security barrier that seals off Israel.

Maayan is an 18-year-old Israeli woman from Adi, a small community in northern Israel. She decided to put off her required military service in order to volunteer in Magen David Adom (MDA). MDA is Israel's equivalent to the Red Cross. Maayan is a paramedic giving first-aid treatment to injured and sick patients.

Maayan studied in an agricultural school near her home. The school has a dairy barn and a horse ranch. Maayan completed the school's horse care program, and she enjoys riding horses. She loves the landscapes of her childhood, and does not think she would like to live in the city. Still, not everything is peaceful and quiet in the region where she grew up. Israel faces the threat of terrorist attack.

HORSEBACK RIDING
Maayan enjoys riding and caring for her horse.

TRADITIONAL MUSIC
Muhammad is learning to play the *oud*, a traditional stringed instrument, in music school.

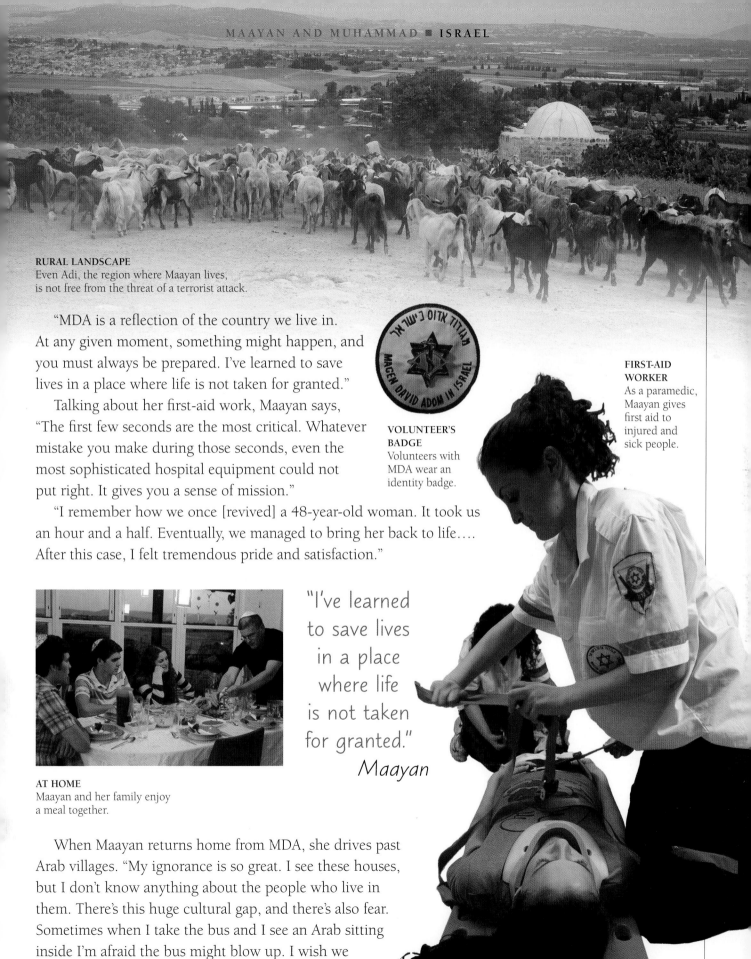

RURAL LANDSCAPE
Even Adi, the region where Maayan lives,
is not free from the threat of a terrorist attack.

"MDA is a reflection of the country we live in. At any given moment, something might happen, and you must always be prepared. I've learned to save lives in a place where life is not taken for granted."

Talking about her first-aid work, Maayan says, "The first few seconds are the most critical. Whatever mistake you make during those seconds, even the most sophisticated hospital equipment could not put right. It gives you a sense of mission."

"I remember how we once [revived] a 48-year-old woman. It took us an hour and a half. Eventually, we managed to bring her back to life…. After this case, I felt tremendous pride and satisfaction."

VOLUNTEER'S BADGE
Volunteers with MDA wear an identity badge.

FIRST-AID WORKER
As a paramedic, Maayan gives first aid to injured and sick people.

"I've learned to save lives in a place where life is not taken for granted."
Maayan

AT HOME
Maayan and her family enjoy a meal together.

When Maayan returns home from MDA, she drives past Arab villages. "My ignorance is so great. I see these houses, but I don't know anything about the people who live in them. There's this huge cultural gap, and there's also fear. Sometimes when I take the bus and I see an Arab sitting inside I'm afraid the bus might blow up. I wish we didn't live in a conflict, but you have to learn a lot about the other side and get to know it."

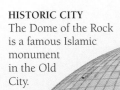

HISTORIC CITY
The Dome of the Rock is a famous Islamic monument in the Old City.

Fifteen-year-old Muhammad likes to walk the narrow streets of the Old City of Jerusalem where he was born. Muhammad lives in a Jerusalem neighborhood called Beit Safafa. His family has been living here for many generations. It was built by two large families, or clans, and Muhammad's is one of them. Like Maayan, Muhammad enjoys horseback riding. "I particularly like to ride my cousins' horses.... I am sure I'd like to spend the rest of my life in Beit Safafa."

Muhammad is a Muslim living in Israel as part of its Arab minority. Both he and his family have many Arab Palestinian friends and acquaintances living in the Israeli-controlled West Bank.

WEST BANK BARRIER
The wall that separates Israelis and Palestinians in Jerusalem is patrolled by Israeli guards.

Seven years ago, Israel built a wall near Muhammad's home—part of the West Bank Security Barrier—to try to prevent terrorist attacks on Israel. Muhammad doesn't like the barrier, because security restrictions make it difficult or impossible to cross. Those who do cross may have difficulty returning. Muhammad says, "I still remember how we used to walk to Bethlehem, which is only two miles away.... Some people in my neighborhood are Israeli Arabs whose partners are Palestinian. Because of the barrier, they cannot meet now."

A WOODEN OUD
The *oud* is a commonly played instrument in Middle Eastern music.

SHARING A MEAL
Muhammad discusses his life
in Jerusalem over food.

Muhammad is
learning to play the
oud (ood), a traditional
pear-shaped wooden
stringed instrument, in
a music school not far
from the Old City. Both
Arabs and Jews attend
this school. Muhammad
plays traditional Arab music. In
the school, he joined a Jewish-Arab
youth orchestra, with 25 musicians. They play
original adaptations of traditional Arab music and
combinations of eastern and western musical styles.

*"In our music school, there are
both Jewish and Arab teachers.
This orchestra is proof
we can coexist."*

Muhammad

STREET STALL
Food stalls are a common sight
around the Old City.

"I don't really care about the conflict. Only human beings
are important to me. In music, there are no Arabs or Jews, only
people playing together and getting to know each other. In our
music school, there are both Jewish and Arab teachers. This
orchestra is proof we can coexist."

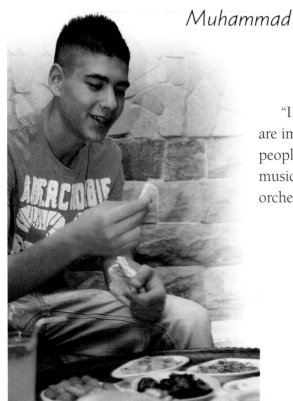

MIDDLE EASTERN FOOD
In the Middle East, a typical meal
consists of many small dishes to share.

Bilal *Turkey*

Bilal lives in Urfa, a city in Turkey. He worries about the future, but believes that Turkey can learn from past mistakes.

Looking out over the rooftops of Urfa, 18-year-old Bilal is proud of his town. This town, located in southeastern Turkey, has been home to Bilal and his family for most of his life.

"Urfa has a very rich history. I want people to come to see Urfa. It is a beautiful place," says Bilal. The city of Urfa is several thousand years old. It was once called Edessa, and was one of the most important cities in the area in ancient times. Like most of Urfa's people, Bilal is a member of the Kurdish ethnic group. He is proud to be both a Kurd and a citizen of the Republic of Turkey.

Kurdish people are a minority in Turkey. For many years, the Turkish government tried to suppress Kurdish culture. Kurds were not allowed to speak the Kurdish language or even give their children Kurdish names. Many Kurds fought the Turkish government because of this. Some still do, although today the government treats Kurdish people better.

HIGH SCHOOL
Because of his work commitments,
Bilal attends school in the afternoons.

Bilal believes that Turks and Kurds are getting along well in Turkey today. "Kurds have been living here for many years. Turks and Kurds have fought in wars together side by side. There are no problems between the Kurds and Turks."

TEA TIME
Before school, Bilal serves tea in a hospital.

HISTORY CLASS
Bilal enjoys studying history because it helps him to understand the recent past and prepare for the future.

OUTSKIRTS OF URFA
Urfa is an ancient city with a rich history.

Bilal speaks Kurdish with his parents and Turkish with his four brothers and two sisters.

"Turkish has become so widespread," he explains. "Older Kurds did not speak much Turkish, but today we speak more Turkish than Kurdish. Turkish is much more useful."

Bilal has been working since he was nine years old. He goes to school as well. "I work and go to school because it is necessary. In the morning I work in the tea house of a hospital. I serve tea. I go to school in the afternoon."

"Urfa has a very rich history.
I want people to come to see Urfa.
It is a beautiful place."
Bilal

Bilal's father works day jobs during the winter and grows pistachios in the summer. "There are a lot of pistachios grown in this part of Turkey," Bilal adds with a smile. "I work on the farm all summer when I am not at school."

Bilal's family has only a small plot of land, so they mainly work in his uncle's field. Lack of water is a constant problem on the farm and across Turkey.

PISTACHIO TREES
In the summer, Bilal's father grows pistachios, which grow well in this dry region.

FIELD WORK
Bilal works in his uncle's field in summer when he is not at school.

"Turkey is surrounded by sea, but salt water is useless," Bilal notes. "Drinking water is scarce. There will be conflict over water. Something must be done about that."

Bilal is concerned about some of the things that lie ahead for his country. He follows current events closely by reading newspapers on the Internet.

WELL CONNECTED
The Internet is an important source of news for Bilal.

"I read the Internet every day," he says. "If we want to see ahead, we have to learn from mistakes and try not repeat them."

WATER SHORTAGE
Drinking water is scarce in Turkey, and Bilal worries that this will cause conflict in the future.

Though Bilal worries about the future, he is encouraged by the progress he has already seen. Urfa's new mayor has brought about many changes to the city, according to Bilal.

"The roads here were awful. My younger brothers and sisters always would come home covered in mud. The mayor fixed the roads. He built new green parks and gardens. I believe he will win again next time around."

FAMILY MEAL
For the family meal, Bilal's mother prepares several different dishes.

"I would like to be a historian. As you investigate the distant past, eventually you come to the recent past. When you study the recent past, you can use it to see ahead."
Bilal

FEEDING THE FISH
Bilal feeds the fish in the courtyard of the mosque of Abd ar-Rahman in Urfa.

Bilal really looks forward to his weekends. "I spend most of my time playing soccer. Like everyone else, everywhere, we like to listen to music and play football." A few years ago, Bilal even made plans to move to Istanbul and become a professional soccer player.

"Back then I thought I wanted to be a soccer player," he laughs. "But as time goes by people change. At one time I wanted to become an engineer, but it was not possible. Now I would like to be a historian. As you investigate the distant past, eventually you come to the recent past. When you study the recent past, you can use it to see ahead."

Askar *Kyrgyzstan*

Askar leads a traditional way of life in the mountains of Kyrgyzstan, Central Asia. He wants to study medicine in the capital, Bishkek, and to use his skills as a doctor to serve his community.

This morning, Askar eats two raw eggs, drinks a glass of milk, puts on his ceremonial clothes, and begins to chant lines from the Epic of Manas. This ancient poem tells the story of a legendary hero called Manas, who fought to save the Kyrgyz people and their homeland.

Like his brothers before him, Askar is trying to memorize what may be the world's longest poem. The Epic of Manas has about half a million lines and would take anywhere from 36 hours to 3 weeks to recite. It seems like an impossible task, but this hasn't stopped Askar from trying. Kyrgyz men take part every year in competitions reciting the poem.

Askar explains, "If it hadn't been for our ancestor Manas, we would have been enslaved as a nation." Today, Manas is a symbol of Kyrgyz pride.

POETRY RECITAL
Askar rehearses lines from the Epic of Manas, an ancient poem about a legendary hero who liberated the Kyrgyz people.

MOUNTAIN TOWN
Askar lives in Naryn, a small town
in the Tian Shan Mountains.

Besides memorizing the
Manas poem, Askar has a
number of other interests. Like
most Kyrgyz boys, horseback
riding is at the top of the list.
He also likes fishing, skiing,
playing an electronic keyboard,
and singing and dancing the
waltz at school. In the winter,
he helps his father to feed the
livestock, and in the summer he
goes to stay with a relative and helps
pick apples and apricots.

"If it hadn't been for our
ancestor Manas, we would have
been enslaved as a nation."
Askar

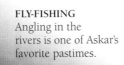

FLY-FISHING
Angling in the
rivers is one of Askar's
favorite pastimes.

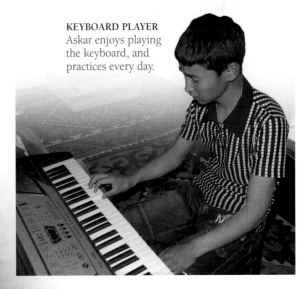

KEYBOARD PLAYER
Askar enjoys playing
the keyboard, and
practices every day.

It is a tradition among the Kyrgyz people
for the youngest son to look after and live
with his grandparents—on his father's
side—when he grows up. As the youngest
of five brothers, this duty falls on Askar's
shoulders. When his uncle is not at home to
take care of his grandparents, Askar goes and
helps. He cleans the house, brings in water
and firewood, and takes care of anything else.

Askar's town is located in the Central Tian Shan Mountains. It is the coldest part of the country, with temperatures falling as low as -40°F. Askar likes living there, but is disturbed by the problems he and his neighbors face.

He believes that water is the most pressing problem. "In the villages there is no clean water to drink," he says. Furthermore, in winter, the water pipes freeze and the villagers have no running water in their homes. They have no choice but to carry water to their homes from a nearby spring. Given the extremely cold weather, some villagers must depend on their neighbors to bring them their drinking water.

"In the villages there is no clean water to drink."
Askar

MOUNTAIN TOWN
Askar's home is in the mountains, where winter temperatures fall well below freezing.

COLLECTING WATER
Askar has to collect water in a large barrel for his family.

But water is not the only problem these mountain people have to deal with. Despite the country's many hydropower plants, Askar was unable to attend school for two months last year because there wasn't enough electricity to keep the schools warm and lighted. Askar says the government told them that they couldn't provide all of Kyrgyzstan with electricity because there was a shortage of water at the power plants. Given Kyrgyzstan's plentiful water supply, Askar believes that the government should do a better job of providing a steady supply of electricity.

SCHOOL DANCE
Askar dances with a classmate at celebrations to mark the last day of the school year.

FAMILY MEAL
Askar and his family often eat meals together.

After graduating from high school, Askar wants to go to medical school and become a doctor. He would like to work in a big city like Bishkek, the capital of Kyrgyzstan, for a year or two. Then he plans to return home, or to one of the mountain villages, to serve his community as a skilled doctor.

SCHOOL BELL
As part of the celebrations to mark the last day of school, students make a huge bell from colored paper.

FINE HORSEMAN
Like many Kyrgyz boys, Askar enjoys horseback riding.

Nancy *India*

This story features Nancy, a young woman who is helping her mother and other local women to start a new business in a mountainous region of India. Eventually, she might study computer science or join the police force.

It is a busy time in Nancy's hometown near Palampur, India. Next week there will be a big wedding, but in the meantime there's plenty of other work to do. Nancy already has many daily chores. She gathers food for the cattle, cleans the house, and even helps her grandfather repair her home. Now that she is 18, she has also joined the Samriddhi, a business run by a group of local women. The women of the Samriddhi work together to harvest, prepare, and sell pickled fruit products. They have one of the few successful businesses in the area.

Palampur lies within a region known as the Changar belt. This is a dry, rocky area marked by ravines and gullies with a scattering of trees that provide shade and color the hills a dusty green. It is a challenging place to earn a living. The land is difficult to farm, but the women of the Samriddhi have found a way to take advantage of local resources.

SUCCESSFUL BUSINESS
The women of the Samriddhi put labels on their jars of pickled produce.

Changar forests are rich with wild fruits. Many of these fruits can be used to make jams and chutney. A chutney is a relish made of fruits mixed with other ingredients such as vinegar and lemon juice.

FAMILY MEAL
Nancy prepares the vegetables for the family meal.

MOUNTAINOUS REGION
Nancy's home is in the foothills of the Himalayas.

"If there is a chance for me to join the police then I will do that. I want to serve my country."
Nancy

WASHING CLOTHES
Nancy and her aunt wash clothes with water from the local hand pump.

"We have many different varieties of fruit…we have lemon, limes, Indian Gooseberry, jackfruit, bamboo shoots, mango, bitter gourds…." explains Nancy, gesturing to a range of Samriddhi jams and chutneys. The whole operation is funded by small bank loans, called microcredit loans. Thanks to these low-risk loans, the Samriddhi women are able to buy the salt, spices, and sugar needed for pickling. They can also use the money for minor expenses such as renting a truck to transport their products to the Samriddhi office.

FEEDING COWS
One of Nancy's daily chores is tending the cows.

ON THE WAY TO THE BANK
Some of the Samriddhi women travel
to the bank to ask for a loan.

Today, Nancy is traveling with her mother and a
few other Samriddhi women to the bank to apply for
a new microcredit loan. "We need a loan so we can
start a plantation. We want to grow some new fruit
trees," Nancy says as we walk along the dusty street
to the small local bank. "It will cost us about 80,000
to 90,000 rupees," she adds, which is about $1,800.

The bank has different payment plans for different
kinds of microloans. The bank manager explains
to Nancy and the group that for a plantation loan,
they need to show that they have plans to clear and
level the land. They will also need to make a down
payment of 15 percent of the total cost of the project.
The rest of the project will be financed by the bank.
Loans for things such as seeds or fertilizer require
a 7 percent down payment.
The money involved may not
seem like much by Western
standards, but the
average annual income
in the region is only
about $300 a year.

LEMON PICKLE
Nancy and her
aunt prepare
lemons for
pickling.

CUTTING FODDER
Nancy climbs a tree to cut
fodder for the animals.

Nancy is proud to be involved in the process and excited about helping to set up a new plantation. The older women are glad to have Nancy in the group as well. They know she is high-spirited, hardworking, and intelligent.

Later, Nancy and her mother prepare for a week-long sales trip. They fill the sales van with their products and set off. Their first stop is just outside Palampur itself, but they will also travel to several other towns before returning home.

Nancy works hard to sell as much as she can. She knows that the money they make will not only help pay for the new loan, but also provide income for her family. Some of the money will be set aside to educate Nancy and her brother. "Right now I am planning to study computer science," Nancy says. "But if there is a chance for me to join the police then I will do that. I want to serve my country."

By working together to manage the land and grow a business, the Samriddhi has brought the community together.

SALES TRIP
Nancy and her mother fill the van with their products in preparation for a sales trip.

The Samriddhi has done more for this village than just make money, it has provided hope for the future. By working together to manage the land and grow a business, the Samriddhi has brought the community together. Sometime soon they hope to see fruit growing on the new plantation that Nancy and the microcredit loan help set up. That will be something for everyone to enjoy!

FRUIT TREE PLANTATION
Nancy, her mother, and her aunt walk in a plantation of young trees that will one day yield fruit for making pickles.

CEMENT CARRIER
Nancy even helps to repair her family home.

Xiao *China*

Xiao is a young man who lives in China where life is changing rapidly. He cares for his family and the environment.

Xiao lives with his father, mother, grandmother, and older brother in a tiny village near Wuxi (woo shee), an ancient city in the east of China. After learning of his father's diabetes diagnosis, 17-year-old Xiao found a full-time job to help support his family. Xiao (whose name is pronounced show, as in *shower*) and his brother both work at a factory that produces machines that make ice cream. His mother works at a different factory and tends the family's orange and peach orchard. His father is a part-time driver.

Every morning at 7 A.M., Xiao rides his motorcycle to Wuxi. There are many factories in this area. They have easy access to railways and canals that transport goods to large cities, such as Shanghai. Xiao works 10 hours a day, five days a week. Many local youth leave to make their fortunes, but Xiao wants to stay close to his family.

DAILY COMMUTE
Xiao travels to and from work on his motorbike.

XIAO'S VILLAGE
Many houses in Xiao's
village are being repaired.

"If the environment is better,
people behave better."
Xiao

Life has changed as China has become wealthier. Meat used to be too expensive to eat every day. Thirty years ago, few people could afford a television. Now, most families in Xiao's village own one.

Unlike his parents' generation, which suffered famine and shortages of many goods, Xiao doesn't remember a time when food was scarce.

He does remember when the waters of Lake Tai were clean and clear. Lake Tai is China's third-largest body of fresh water. It is just a five-minute walk from Xiao's house. As a boy, he learned to swim there. He collected snails in the lake and had mud fights with friends.

FAMILY CHEF
Xiao's mother cooks fish
and vegetables for the
family using a large wok.

LAKE TAI
The waters of Lake Tai used to be clean and clear but are now polluted.

Walking through the family's fruit orchard, it's hard to imagine this place ever smelled like anything other than sun-ripened oranges. Yet in the summer of 2007 a terrible odor crept from the lake across the orchard and into their home.

An algae bloom covered the lake with green slime. The algae bloom was caused, in part, by pollution and pesticides from the farms and factories around the lake. The algae used up the oxygen in the lake. Suffocated fish floated to the surface, belly up.

"You didn't even want to use the water to bathe, much less to drink," says Xiao.

FRUIT ORCHARD
Xiao's mother applies pesticides to the orange trees in their orchard.

ALGAE PATROL
Local people hire professionals to clean up the algae from the lake.

Thirty million people rely on Lake Tai for drinking water. That summer, families in Xiao's village avoided the lake water. They drew water from local wells or bought bottles of water. Bottled water was rushed to Wuxi during the crisis.

Xiao's family shut the windows and put up with the stench. Flies and mosquitoes swarmed.

BOILING WATER
Xiao boils water to make
it safe to drink.

LOCAL POND
Xiao is dismayed by
the trash thrown into
the local pond.

Small ponds where neighbors had once
washed their fruit and rinsed their rice filled
with algae and muck. People started to throw
their garbage into these pools, as well.

"If the environment is better, people behave
better," says Xiao. "When there's pollution, people
throw their garbage where they shouldn't."

The city of Wuxi has started to solve the problem.
They hired people to remove the algae. They have also shut
down some factories around the lake to reduce the pollution.

"How can you choose between
your family and your home?"
Xiao

DEMOLITION
A factory is demolished to prevent
further pollution.

Towns are also being bulldozed. Citizens in the village
next to Xiao's village were forced to move when the
government claimed the area for a park. Xiao has never
lived anywhere else and worries the government will
make his family move, too.

He has mixed feelings about his parent's use of
pesticides and fertilizers in their orchard. He knows these
chemicals run off into the lake and cause more harm. He
also knows that the factory where he works may be adding
to the pollution. Still, Xiao needs his job. He hopes to
save money, marry, and start a family—preferably, he says,
by the time he's 23—so there are no easy answers.

"How can you choose between your family
and your home?"

Asuka *Japan*

Asuka is a senior in high school and lives with her family in the busy city of Yokohama, Japan. She feels she has had a privileged upbringing and that contributed to her wanting to make the world a better place.

In the bamboo- and concrete-covered hills of Yokohama, a cluster of identical apartment blocks stands out. The drab, box-shaped buildings have numbers stenciled onto the top of their walls to identify them. On the third floor of one of the apartment buildings, in a small apartment no bigger than an average American living room, lives Asuka. The third-year high school student shares the apartment with her father, her grandmother, her 15-year-old brother, the family's pet turtle, and Max, a pet rabbit.

FAMILY PET
Asuka has a pet rabbit called Max.

CROWDED HOUSING
Asuka and her family live in a tiny third-floor apartment in a crowded area.

METROPOLIS
Tokyo-Yokohama is one of the most
densely populated areas in the world.

More than 35 million people live in the Greater Tokyo-
Yokohama metropolitan area. This is almost twice as many people
as live in Greater New York. With so many people needing
housing, space is scarce. Most people live in small apartments.
About 2,500 people live in this four-block square area of
Yokohama. It is very crowded, and the cost of living is high.

For a single-parent family, it can be a struggle to make ends
meet. Asuka's family moved to Yokohama after her parents
divorced. She was three years old. To support the family, her
father took a job as a salesman in the construction industry.
With money short, Asuka also helps out by working up to
20 hours a week after school. She gives one third of her wages
to the family and uses the rest to pay her other expenses.

EATING AT HOME
The family eats together
at their kitchen table.

"We can improve the living
conditions of people and
make things better."
Asuka

HOME STUDY
Asuka's brother studies in
a small office at home.

**PACKED
TRAIN**
It is standing
room only
on the train
Asuka takes
to school.

Though her family does not have a lot of money, the 18-year-old high school senior considers herself fortunate. Every day she wakes up at 6:30 A.M., grabs the "bento" lunch box her grandmother has prepared, and heads off to school. She attends a high school in the middle of Yokohama, where she studies international affairs. Her curriculum is demanding. It includes courses in world history, politics, economics, Japanese, English, and Korean.

AT SCHOOL
Asuka and her friends wait for class to begin.

Asuka has developed a keen interest in politics, economics, and history. She plans to major in these subjects when she goes to college. Asuka thinks it is important to study politics and history because it explains how various countries have developed and the way their governments work. With that knowledge, she believes, "we can improve the living conditions of people and make things better."

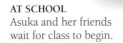
CLUB LEADER
Asuka is leader of the school Glocally Club.

WELL EQUIPPED
The students at Asuka's school have access to modern technology.

Asuka is a high-energy person. In addition to her studies and her job, she takes part in extracurricular activities. These activities range from volunteer work to playing drums in a rock band. Asuka is also the leader of the school's "Glocally" Club. (The club's name is a combination of the words "global" and "locally.") As part of the club's activities, the students go on field trips to observe war ruins. They also learn how wars affect people and look for ways to achieve peace in the modern world.

The teacher in charge of the club has introduced the students to some serious issues that are far from the minds of the average high school student in most developed countries. Asuka is glad he challenges them to think about real-world issues.

Over the last couple of years, Asuka has also taken part in the Yokohama Student Forum. Last year she became a student leader and put together a forum on child labor—an issue that touches the lives of families across Asia.

FIELD TRIP
The Glocally Club goes on field trips to observe war ruins.

MEETING FRIENDS
Asuka takes a break from her many activities to relax with friends.

> "I have [led] a privileged life, while others are suffering elsewhere."
> *Asuka*

Asuka appreciates all the opportunities she has had. "I have [led] a privileged life," she says, "while others are suffering elsewhere." After graduating from college, Asuka says she wants to do something to help others less privileged.

Judging by what she has achieved so far, the promising young student will be sure to put her talents to good use in the future.

PROMISING FUTURE
Asuka wants to use her talents to help others.

Ridwan *Indonesia*

Ridwan helps his family and friends prepare for his cousin's wedding on the island of Sumatra in Indonesia. When Ridwan himself marries, he will move into his wife's home, as is the Minangkabau custom.

Laughing voices drift through the cool air as 19-year-old Ridwan works with the men. They are busily moving furniture and cleaning the house where a wedding ceremony will take place. Meanwhile, in the kitchen, dozens of women are preparing chili peppers, onions, garlic, ginger, and a host of other spices. The spices will go into the meat and vegetable dishes of the day-long wedding feast. Although it is still early in the morning, there is not a moment to lose. Soon hundreds of relatives, friends, and neighbors will start arriving to honor the happy couple getting married today.

Ridwan looks out over the rice fields and the sea that surround this village called Bukittinggi, a name meaning "high hill." He can't wait to see his cousin, Nentis, who is the bride, begin her life with Al, her groom.

CHEFS AT WORK
Women prepare the food that is served during the day-long wedding ceremony.

MINANGKABAU HOUSE
Traditional Minangkabau houses have curved
roofs like the horns of a water buffalo.

"Weddings are happy and important events
that everyone looks forward to because it's a time
for relatives and friends to get together. Today is
especially meaningful to me, not only because
my cousin is getting married, but it's also the
first time I've attended a Minangkabau wedding,"
says Ridwan. (The Minangkabau are the main
ethnic group in West Sumatra.) And according to
Minangkabau practice, Al is moving
into Nentis' home, which belongs
to the bride's grandmother.

> "Weddings are happy and
> important events that everyone
> looks forward to."
> *Ridwan*

Minangkabau culture is unique. Minangkabau
houses often have upward-curved roofs that
look like the horns of a water
buffalo. The resemblance
is not a coincidence. For
centuries the Minangkabau
depended on the buffalo
for food and to help them
plow the rice fields. In fact,
the name Minangkabau
means "winning buffalo."
The Minangkabau are also
one of the few ethnic groups
in the world in which family
homes are passed down
from mothers to daughters,
instead of from fathers
to sons.

BRIDE AND GROOM
The happy couple wear
dazzling costumes decorated
with gold thread and jewelry.

WEDDING VENUE
Ridwan arrives at the venue where the
marriage ceremony will take place.

Nentis starts dressing early, because her wedding costume consists of layers of silk and other fabric woven with gold thread, gold jewelry, and a glittering Minangkabau headdress. Meanwhile, Al dons his suit. He looks like an Indian *raja*, or king, as he slips on a *kris*, an ornamental dagger. Such costumes reveal the Chinese and Indian influences that have helped shape Minangkabau culture.

WEDDING GUESTS
Guests come from all over Indonesia to enjoy the wedding feast.

GAMELAN MUSICIAN
At the reception, a group of musicians play *gamalan* music which features traditional instruments like these gong chimes called *bonang*.

Later in the day, as a band plays, the couple moves to the wedding dais. Everyone lines up to congratulate the smiling pair. It is a long day for the couple as they rise repeatedly to greet new arrivals. During the feast, long-separated relatives laugh and exchange news. Many have traveled from distant parts of Indonesia to be here today.

RESPLENDENT
The bride and groom wear several different elaborate costumes during the ceremony.

Traveling and moving away from home are a common practice among the Minangkabau. In fact, Ridwan's parents left Bukittinggi years ago to run a textile shop in East Java. Ridwan helps at his uncle's textile business and lives in his maternal grandmother's house. The house will one day be passed down to Ridwan's mother and aunt, and then to his sister. When the time comes for Ridwan and his brothers to marry, they will move into their wives' homes. It is the Minangkabau way.

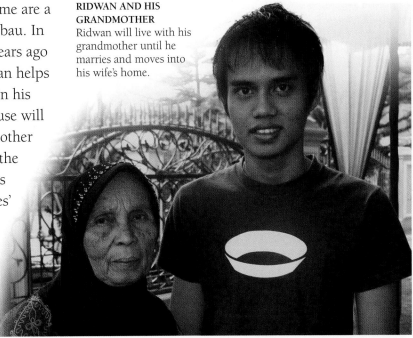

RIDWAN AND HIS GRANDMOTHER
Ridwan will live with his grandmother until he marries and moves into his wife's home.

"I'd like to further my studies in the Indonesian language and be a theater performer."
Ridwan

"This is part of Minangkabau culture and I totally accept it, just as all the other men do. It just makes me work harder at my vocation," says Ridwan. "I'd like to further my studies in the Indonesian language and be a theater performer. My father, of course, hopes I'll take over his business one day, but I think I'll deal with that later," he smiles shyly.

Ridwan returns to his video camera, using modern technology to record an ancient tradition and the scenes that his family will enjoy throughout their lives.

TEXTILE SHOP
Ridwan helps at his uncle's textile business.

VIDEO RECORDING
Ridwan makes a lasting record of the day's events.

A MAN AND HIS HORSE
A skilled horseman, Jack loves performing tricks on horseback.

Jack *New Zealand*

Jack is a 17-year old from New Zealand who is trying to stay connected to his Maori culture. He hopes to become a skilled Maori speaker like his father.

It is early one weekday morning, and 17-year-old Jack is busy getting ready for another day at school. Jack lives in Auckland, New Zealand's largest city. By 7:30 A.M., Jack is on the bus for the 50-minute ride to his school, Avondale College.

Jack lives with his two younger brothers and his mother, father, and grandmother. Jack's father is a television actor and comedian. His mother manages the household and works in a television production company.

Jack is part Maori (MAOW ree), descended from the original inhabitants of New Zealand. The Maori migrated to New Zealand—which they call Aotearoa (AOW tee AR roh uh)—from other parts of the Pacific region about 1,000 years ago.

MAORI CARVING
Jack wears a Maori pendant around his neck.

FAMILY HOME
Jack and his family live in a modern house surrounded by parkland.

AUCKLAND
Located on the North Island of New Zealand, Auckland is a large modern metropolis.

Maori students make up about 8 percent of the 2,600 students at Avondale College. They have their own *wharenui* (meeting house) and *wharekai* (dining hall) at school. At breaks, lunchtimes, and after school, Maori students gather at the wharekai to talk and share food with friends.

But Maori people like Jack and his friends once faced many obstacles in New Zealand. During the 1800s, British colonization of New Zealand led to a series of wars with the Maori. Many Maoris moved to cities and lost touch with their culture.

MAORI STUDENTS
At Avondale College, Maori students like Jack have their own meeting house and dining hall.

"I know the blood of my ancestors is in that soil."
Jack

BOY BAND
Jack and his two younger brothers have fun playing music together.

91

Interest in Maori culture has grown since the mid-1900s. Today, many Maori study their language, history, and customs. Jack feels a strong connection to his culture and to his homeland on New Zealand's North Island. "I know the blood of my ancestors is in that soil," he says quietly, "because they gave their lives fighting for that land."

MAORI CARVING
This carving shows the aggressive posture that Jack practices.

"If you are interested, it's a lot easier to learn."
Jack

IN CLASS
Jack and his classmates are serious about their school studies.

Jack takes a Maori language class at school every day. He hopes to become a skilled Maori speaker like his father, who grew up speaking Maori. Although Jack went to a Maori-language day care center as a child, his parents decided to send him to English-language schools. English is the language most commonly spoken in New Zealand. At home, the family speaks English.

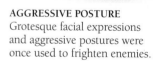

AGGRESSIVE POSTURE
Grotesque facial expressions and aggressive postures were once used to frighten enemies.

Jack stays connected to Maori culture in other ways. He is one of the leaders of his school's *kapa haka* team. Kapa haka is a performance art that combines singing and dancing. It uses parts of traditional Maori songs, dances, and combat techniques.

KAPA HAKA TEAM
Jack and his high-school class practice for the national kapa haka competition.

POLYNESIAN CANOES
As a member of the school waka ama team, Jack practices canoeing on the open ocean.

CANOEING TEAM
The team waits in line for their turn to get into the canoes.

Each year, New Zealand holds a national competition for high-school students of kapa haka. This competition is part of Polyfest, a celebration of Polynesian culture and dance. To prepare for the competition, Jack's kapa haka team practices each day at lunchtime and after school. It also practices for at least one full day each weekend.

Jack is also a member of his school's *waka ama* team. Waka ama are Maori canoes designed for use on the open ocean. Avondale has male, female, and mixed waka ama teams. Students of all ethnic backgrounds take part in the sport.

Jack plans to continue studying the Maori language and participating in kapa haka after he finishes school. He hopes to increase his understanding of his culture. "If you're interested, it's a lot easier to learn," Jack says. "There are a lot of people out there who have the knowledge. You've just got to be willing to go out and grab it."

FUTURE PLANS
Jack intends to increase his understanding of the Maori culture.

Index

Acknowledgments

The people who made up the team on location—representing producers, camera and photography, journalists, and location managers—are listed below:

Munir Akdogan, Jorge Alborta, Danya M. Alhamrani, Shiri Bar-On, Hila Baroz, Chris Brokensha, Neville Cole, Michael Condon, Heath Cozens, Aniruddha Das, Raquel Dias, Can Ertür, Greg Fell, Travis Hamilton, David House, Rodrigo House, Bruce Jarvis, Jake Johnson, Cory Kirk, Dima Kolchinsky, Stephanie Kovak, Dean Leslie, Bindu Mathur, Cesar Nan Num, Dania Nassief, Chrispat Okutu, Oyton Orgul, Millie Phuah, John "Freddie" Quicero, Markian Radiovich, Paul Ramirez, Richard Rapp, Tui Ruwhiu, Dmitry Saltykovskiy, Megan Shank, Sachin Singh, Stephanie Smith, Carl Thelin, Anthony Trotter, Miguel Vassy, Wes White, Oliver Wilkins, Greg Windley.

The people who made up the Pearson Prentice Hall in-house *myWorld Geography* team—representing composition services, core design digital and multimedia production services, digital product development, editorial, editorial services, manufacturing, marketing, and production management—are listed below:

Leann Davis Alspaugh, Sarah Aubry, Deanna Babikian, Paul Blankman, Alyssa Boehm, Peter Brooks, Susan Brorein, Megan Burnett, Todd Christy, Neville Cole, Bob Craton, Michael Di Maria, Glenn Diedrich, Frederick Fellows, Jorgensen Fernandez, Thomas Ferreira, Patricia Fromkin, Andrea Golden, Mary Ann Gundersen, Christopher Harris, Susan Hersch, Paul Hughes, Judie Jozokos, John Kingston, Kate Koch, Stephanie Krol, Karen Lepri, Ann-Michelle Levangie, Salena LiBritz, Courtney Markham, Constance J. McCarty, Anne McLaughlin, Rich McMahon, Mark O'Malley, Alison Muff, Jen Paley, Gabriela Perez Fiato, Judith Pinkham, Paul Ramos, Charlene Rimsa, Marcy Rose, Rashid Ross, Alexandra Sherman, Owen Shows, Melissa Shustyk, Jewel Simmons, Ted Smykal, Emily Soltanoff, Frank Tangredi, Simon Tuchman, Elizabeth Tustian, Merle Uuesoo, Alwyn Velásquez, Andrew White, Heather Wright.